BIGGEST BOOK OF THE HUMAN BODY

Text by
Vanessa Giancamilli Birch, Laura Gates Galvin, Sarah Kincius, Esther Reisberg, Isabella Simon

Photo Credits
Dreamstime, iClipart, iStockphoto

Kidsbooks®

Visit us at www.kidsbooks.com

Get ready to learn about
the amazing

HUMAN BODY!

Find out:

- Which muscle never gets tired
- Why your ears pop when you're on an airplane
- Fun ways to move your body
- What the human body has in common with other animal bodies
- How your body parts work as a team to keep you healthy

And much, much more!

Also includes Search & Find® puzzles, mazes, word searches, and other fun activities!

Get ready to impress your family and friends with your knowledge of the human body!

Kidsbooks®

Your Body Is Amazing!

The average human body has 78 organs, which are groups of tissues working together to perform functions in the body. These organs are grouped into 11 major organ systems: circulatory, digestive, endocrine, immune, nervous, muscular, skeletal, reproductive, respiratory, urinary, and integumentary.

If you unraveled a human being's DNA, it would measure 10 billion miles—about the distance from Earth to Pluto and back!

THE BODY OF AN ADULT HUMAN IS MADE UP OF ABOUT 7 OCTILLION ATOMS, TINY PARTICLES THAT MAKE UP ALL MATTER.

Unless you have a **TWIN**, the way you look is **UNIQUE!**

When you are awake, your brain produces enough energy to light up a small light bulb.

SPECIAL CELLS IN YOUR SKIN PRODUCE VITAMIN D WHEN YOUR BODY IS EXPOSED TO SUNLIGHT.

YOUR **BRAIN** IS MORE ACTIVE AT **NIGHT** THAN DURING THE DAY.

Each **person** has unique **fingerprints** and a unique **tongue print.**

The human brain can read up to 1,000 words per minute, but only speed-readers can read this fast. Most people are able to read 250 words per minute.

GRAVITY MAKES OUR **EARS** AND NOSES DROOP THROUGHOUT OUR LIVES, CREATING THE ILLUSION THAT THEY ARE ALWAYS GROWING.

The muscles that move your fingers are actually in your palms. Your fingers have muscles, too, but they only work to make the hairs on your fingers stand up—creating goose bumps.

YOUR BODY IS MADE UP MOSTLY OF **WATER.**

Systems of the Body
Muscular System

Big Responsibility

The muscular system is responsible for daily functions such as movement, circulating blood, and helping to maintain posture. This system consists of over 650 muscles.

MUSCLE MEMORY

Muscle memory is formed when the body repeats an action over and over again. Muscle memory allows the body to get better at a certain activity, as muscles train themselves to become more precise and accurate in their motions.

Don't Think About It

Some of your muscle groups are involuntary, meaning you do not have to think about controlling them; they go to work on their own! Cardiac muscle, which is in your heart, is involuntary, as is smooth muscle. Smooth muscle is found on the walls of your stomach, esophagus, intestines, and bladder, as well as your blood vessels and other organs and structures in the body. Skeletal muscles are the only voluntary group, and those are the muscles that control actions you do on purpose, like walking.

TEARING IT UP

We are born with the same number of muscle fibers we will have our whole lives. When we exercise, our muscles tear down and grow back thicker, causing muscles to get bigger and stronger.

Working for You

Muscles work hard! The muscular system uses 200 muscles to take a single step. The heart is the hardest working muscle in the body. The muscles in your eyes are some of the busiest: When you read for as little as one hour, your eyes make about 10,000 coordinated movements.

Don't Push Me

Muscles can only pull, not push. For example, the arm is able to push a door open because the muscles in the back of the arm pull on the elbow. If every muscle in your body could pull in the same direction, they would create a force of 25 tons!

Making Sense of Your Five Senses

Sensational

Senses are your body's reactions to physical experiences in the world around you. They are made up of a collection of sensory organs or cells that relay information to the brain, which the brain interprets, or makes sense of, and creates a response.

COMMON SENSES

It is largely agreed that humans have five main senses: sight, hearing, taste, touch, and smell. They are controlled by five main sense organs: eyes, ears, tongue, skin, and nose.

Sensing Scents

Smell and taste are chemical senses. We have hundreds of olfactory, or smell, receptors in our nose, and each one binds to its own separate molecular smell feature.

DID YOU KNOW?

About 80% of what we think is taste is actually smell. Flavor is a mix of taste and smell perception. If you hold your nose when you eat, you probably won't be able to taste your food very well!

What a Sight!

Your eyes can process 36,000 bits of information per hour and will process about 24 million images in your lifetime. Around 85% of your knowledge comes from what you see. Because your eyes are so efficient at translating the things you see into data the brain can process, you are able to understand visual information instantly, allowing you to react and respond to your environment.

Touchy Subject

Touch is activated by nerve endings on the skin, such as hair follicles, as well as pressure receptors in the throat and on the tongue. These receptors send information to the brain using small electrical impulses, which travel up the spinal cord and tell you whether something is cold or hot, smooth or rough. The four primary receptors sending information to your brain are chemoreceptors (chemical changes), mechanoreceptors (pressure), photoreceptors (light), and thermoreceptors (temperature).

Sounds Good

Sound is measured in decibels (dB). Normal conversation is about 60 dB. Sounds above 85 dB are harmful, depending on how often and for how long you are exposed to the noise. At 120 dB, which is the noise level you would hear standing in front of the speakers at a rock concert with no ear protection, you could experience instantaneous, or immediate, hearing loss.

Every Breath You Take
The Lungs

Precious Cargo

The main job of your lungs is to transport oxygen from the air you inhale into your bloodstream. At the same time, your lungs remove carbon dioxide from your body, which is released into the air when you exhale.

NO SMOKING

IN ADDITION TO BEING BAD FOR YOUR GENERAL HEALTH, SMOKING IS BAD FOR YOUR LUNGS. SMOKING CAN CAUSE LUNG CANCER AND OTHER DISEASES THAT AFFECT THE LUNGS, AS WELL AS THROAT AND MOUTH CANCERS.

STUDY UP

The study of lung diseases is called pulmonology. Common lung diseases include asthma, pneumonia, and bronchitis. Other lung diseases include emphysema, tuberculosis, and lung cancer.

Holding Your Breath

Your maximum lung capacity—how much air your lungs can hold—is about 6 liters, or three large soda bottles. By the time you are 25, your lungs will be fully mature. After you turn 35, lung function declines and, over time, breathing can become more difficult. People who have a large lung capacity can send oxygen around their bodies faster. You can increase your lung capacity with regular exercise.

Narrow Airways

Asthma is a lung disease that causes the airways to narrow, swell, and create extra mucus. Asthma attacks happen when airways get irritated and symptoms get worse, causing coughing and wheezing and making it hard to breathe in air.

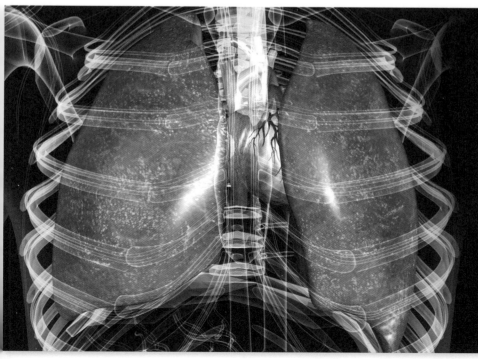

Not Like the Other

Humans have two lungs, and the lung on the right side of your body is not exactly the same as the lung on the left side. Your left lung has two lobes, and your right lung has three. Your left lung is slightly smaller than your right, leaving room for your heart. You can live with only one lung, though it might limit your physical ability in certain ways.

Heart of the Matter

Pump It Up

The heart is a muscle in the middle of the chest, between the lungs, that pushes blood through the body like a pump. The heart pumps about 2,000 gallons of blood through the blood vessels every day.

Beat of My Heart

The average human heart beats 60 to 100 times per minute, but your heart rate lowers when you are asleep, sometimes dipping down to around 40 beats per minute. This happens because your metabolism slows and your parasympathetic nervous system—also known as the "rest and digest" system—is more active, allowing your heart to slow and your body to relax.

The Heart Will Go On

In your lifetime, your heart will pump about 200 train tank cars full of blood, and—as long as there is an adequate supply of oxygen—the human heart can continue to beat when it is removed from the body.

HEARTFELT RHYTHM

By the time you are an adult, your heart is about the size of a grapefruit.

The sound you hear when you listen to a heartbeat is from the four heart valves closing. You can feel your heartbeat on your wrist and on either side of your throat, and your heartbeat can change to mimic the music you are listening to.

THE HEART

weighs between 7 and 15 ounces, about the same weight as a bottle of ketchup.

DID YOU KNOW?

Women's hearts beat faster than men's, but men have larger hearts. While both genders experience heart attacks, the symptoms are different in women and men: Men may sweat and feel chest pain; women may experience dizziness, shortness of breath, and upper back pressure.

Systems of the Body
Nervous System

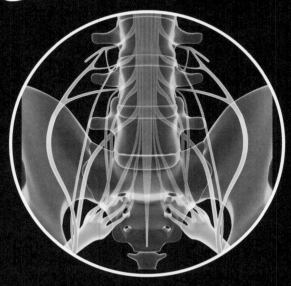

It Takes Nerve

The nervous system includes the brain, spinal cord, and a network of nerve cells, or neurons. This system acts as the body's control center, sending messages from the brain throughout the body, and is responsible for all your actions and reactions. It's thanks to the nervous system that you pull your hand back when you accidentally touch a hot stove or get up to answer the door when you hear the doorbell ring!

IN CONTROL

The nervous system is made up of the central nervous system (CNS) and the peripheral nervous system (PNS). The CNS is made up of the brain and the spinal cord. The PNS includes the nerve fibers that branch off from the spinal cord and extend to the rest of the body, including the neck, torso, arms, legs, muscles, and internal organs.

High-speed Connection

The brain, spinal cord, and nerves consist of more than 100 billion nerve cells. These cells transmit messages to your brain at a speed of about 180 miles per hour!

Brain Maze
Think It Through

The human brain looks like it has hills and valleys over its surface. See if you can navigate up, down, and around the uneven terrain of the brain to get from one side to the other!

START

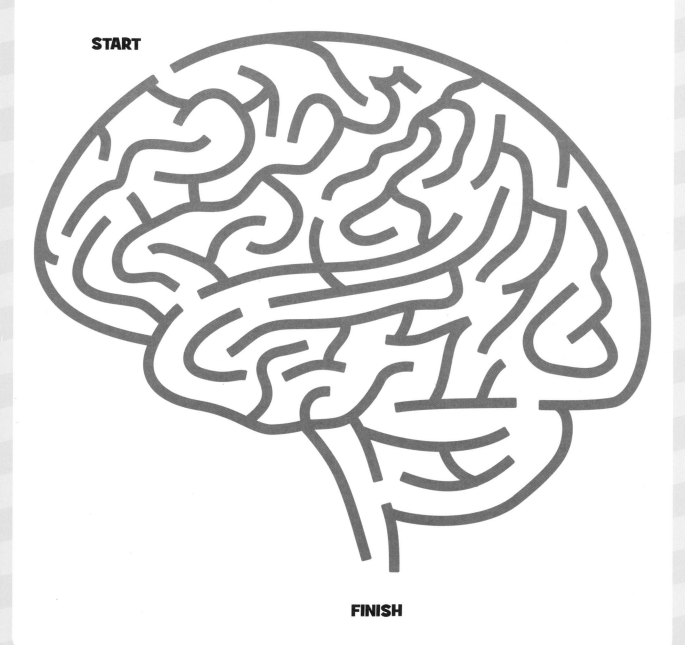

FINISH

Answer on page 298

Down to the Bone

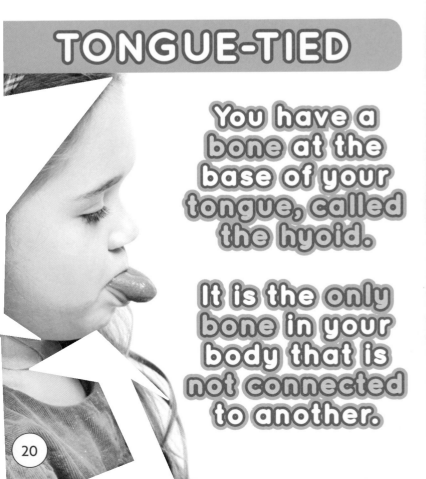

YOUR FUNNY BONE IS ACTUALLY A NERVE CALLED THE ULNAR NERVE. IT GETS ITS NICKNAME FROM THE FUNNY TINGLE CAUSED BY HITTING IT.

TONGUE-TIED

You have a bone at the base of your tongue, called the hyoid.

It is the only bone in your body that is not connected to another.

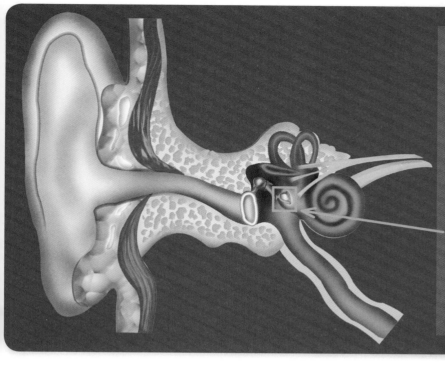

HAVE YOU HEARD?

THE
SMALLEST BONE
IN YOUR BODY IS
INSIDE YOUR EAR.

IT'S CALLED THE
STAPES OR STIRRUP,
AND IT'S ABOUT THE **SIZE** OF
A **GRAIN** OF **RICE**.

Making Connections

Joints are the areas where our bones meet (see pages 222–223). Ligaments, a type of tissue, and muscles hold bones together at the joints (see pages 248–249). Skeletal muscles are attached to the bones with the help of tendons, which work as special connectors between muscle and bone (see pages 180–181).

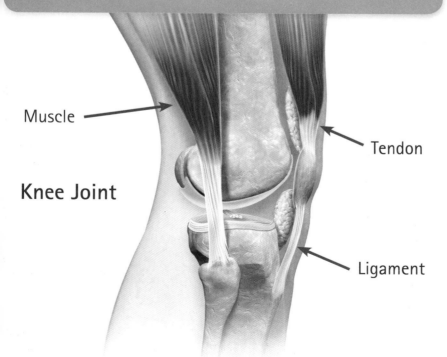

Muscle

Tendon

Knee Joint

Ligament

FLOATING rIBS

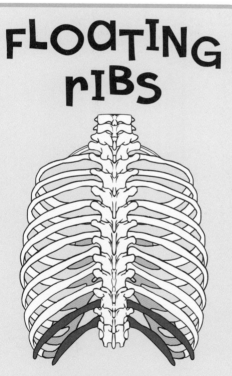

Your last two sets of ribs are called floating ribs. They aren't connected to the ribs above them or to the breastbone. They are, however, attached to the spine in the back, so they won't ever really float away!

Hair Apparent

The hair you see on top of your head is considered dead because there is no activity happening in the strands. The only living part of a hair is the section that grows beneath the skin in an organ called a follicle. Hair pushes from the root through the follicle to where it can be seen above the surface.

Hairy Subject

Hair is one of the defining features that makes humans mammals. People have about the same amount of hair on their bodies as chimpanzees—the hairs on humans are just finer and harder to see.

Every day, we lose about 50 to 100 hairs, but that hair will grow back. The average growth of hair is ½ inch per month.

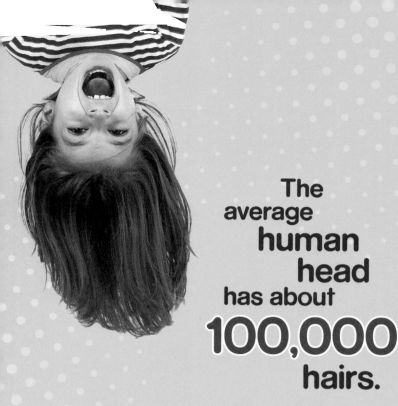

The average **human head** has about **100,000** hairs.

Natural **blondes** have more hair than **brunettes**. Redheads have the least amount of hair.

In-hair-itance

Hair growth is defined by genetics, which means family members pass down genes that control hair color and texture, how much hair you have, and how long it will grow. As far as we know, there is no such thing as male hair or female hair. If a scientist had a strand of human hair, he or she couldn't tell if it came from a male or a female. However, scientists are working on identifying gender by hair samples.

Hair for You

The hair on your head helps keep you warm, and it provides some protection from the sun's UV rays. It's a good idea to wear a hat in the sun to keep your scalp and hair safe from some of the dangers of UV rays. Too much sunlight can dry out hair and make it brittle.

Systems of the Body
Digestive System

BREAK IT DOWN

The digestive system is made up of parts of the body that take in, break down, and absorb food, turning some of it into fuel for the body and removing the waste. Together, the digestive organs are

30 FEET LONG.

On the Outs

The large intestine includes the appendix, cecum, colon, and rectum. It is the final part of the digestive system. It absorbs water from whatever food has not been digested and helps remove unnecessary waste from the body.

Now Processing

The small intestine is where most of the digestion and absorption of food takes place. The stomach sends a thick liquid called chyme into the small intestine, where enzymes continue the digestion process. It takes about 12 hours to completely digest food. Fruits and vegetables can be digested in less than 12 hours, while meat can take up to two or three days.

On average, an adult male's small intestine is 22½ feet long, and a female's is 23 feet long. For both men and women, however, the large intestine is around 5 feet long.

Digestion Helpers

While the stomach and intestines play an important role in digestion, other organs in the body are critical to this system, too. The pancreas secretes the enzymes for the small intestine to use. The liver produces bile used to break down dietary fat, and the gallbladder stores bile.

ACID WASH

The inner wall of the stomach secretes, or produces and gives off, hydrochloric acid, a strong liquid that helps kill bacteria and digest food. This acid is strong enough to dissolve razor blades, so the stomach is lined with a thick coating of mucus for protection. You get a new stomach lining every three to four days. If you didn't, the acids in your tummy would digest your stomach, and you'd basically be eating yourself!

One Smart Cookie
The Brain

Your brain is a wrinkly, pink organ that feels a bit like a soft mushroom.

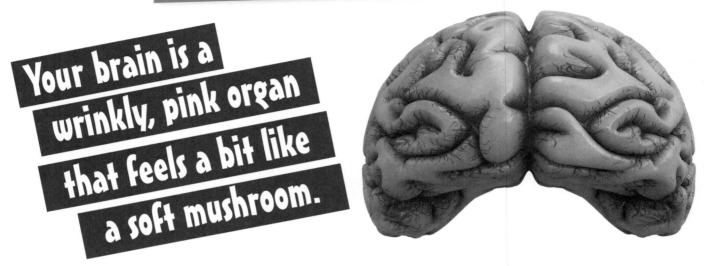

Your brain is the **FATTEST** organ in your body. In fact, the human brain is made of 60% fat. It is also approximately 80% water.

THINK BIG

The brain weighs about 3 pounds, the same as three footballs, which seems like a lot—because it is!

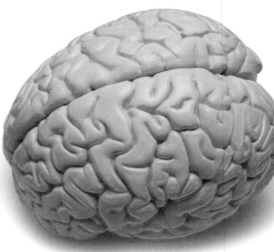

The **human brain** is **two** to **three** times as **big** as the **brain** of other **mammals** that are of a **similar body size.**

NO PAIN

YOUR BRAIN CAN FEEL NO PAIN, BECAUSE IT DOESN'T HAVE PAIN RECEPTORS—BUT THE TISSUES THAT COVER THE BRAIN AND THE BLOOD VESSELS AROUND IT DO. WHEN YOU HAVE A HEADACHE, THE PAIN ISN'T IN YOUR BRAIN—IT IS ACTUALLY FELT BY THE BRAIN'S SURROUNDING MUSCLES AND SKIN.

Brain Freeze

Brain freeze is your brain trying to save you from freezing to death! When your brain recognizes a temperature drop in your mouth, it increases your blood pressure as a way of telling you to slow down to avoid problems that come with dramatic changes in temperature. The scientific term for brain freeze is *sphenopalatine ganglioneuralgia*.

Brain Food

The two most important nutrients to the survival of the brain are oxygen and glucose—without them, the brain can stay alive for three to five minutes before it is permanently damaged. The body will suffer if the brain is damaged because the brain controls the lungs, heart, and consciousness.

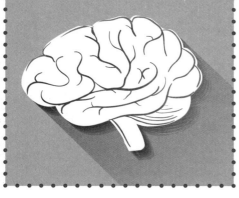

Full of Nerves

The human brain stops growing at about age 18, but the brain will continue to make new neurons, or nerve cells. Researchers believe the brain of an adult can create new nerve cells and absorb them into neural circuits, a necessary process for memory, learning, and stress response. Once brain cells are gone—from aging or extreme lack of sleep, for example—they're gone for good: Brain cells cannot regenerate.

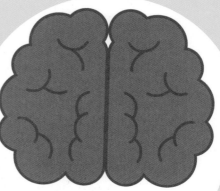

FOOD STAYS IN YOUR STOMACH FOR TWO TO FOUR HOURS.

Your stomach produces up to 3 liters of acid each day.

When you **BLUSH**, the lining of your **STOMACH** blushes, too.

Almost everyone's stomach is about 12 inches long and 6 inches wide. However, people have different food "thermostats," or points at which the stomach tells the brain that it is full.

PEOPLE CAN LIVE WITHOUT A STOMACH IF IT HAS BEEN SURGICALLY REMOVED.

An adult stomach at rest is very small when empty, holding about 7 ounces of stomach acid and bile. However, it can hold almost ½ pound of food at a time if necessary.

Your stomach, with the help of an enzyme called pepsin, helps release the B12 vitamin from the food you eat. B vitamins are important for metabolism and to maintain energy levels.

Spot the Difference

Dinnertime

Find and circle 10 differences between these two pictures of a family about to eat a big meal.

Moving in the Right Direction

I Like to Move It

Exercise helps make you smarter and happier because it causes more blood to flow to your brain. After you exercise, your body creates a chemical that makes your brain more responsive to learning.

Doctors recommend getting at least a half hour of physical activity per day.

FITNESS FACTORS

Exercise improves three key areas of fitness: endurance, strength, and flexibility.

ENDURANCE helps you keep going. You improve endurance by getting your heart rate up for a long time, through aerobic exercise such as running, dancing, and playing soccer.

STRENGTH allows you to climb walls or lift heavy objects. You can get stronger by doing exercises such as push-ups, sit-ups, and pull-ups.

FLEXIBILITY gives your muscles and joints the ability to move easily in a wide range of motion. Doing the splits or even reaching for a book on a shelf helps you stretch and practice flexibility.

Come On, Get Happy

During exercise, your brain releases endorphins, which help lower stress and increase positive emotions, decrease appetite, and improve your immune system, which keeps you from getting sick. Riding a bike, running, or playing—any kind of exercise—makes your body healthy and happy!

Muscling Through

Strength training is important for improving muscle fibers and building muscle. Muscle fibers, which are thinner than human hairs, can support up to 1,000 times their own weight. Strength training works both the muscles and the nervous system, called the neuromuscular system.

Power Saver

A muscle moves by contracting. When your muscles move, you move. Muscle is very efficient, only using about 35% to 50% of its potential energy. It is also good at burning calories—about three times better than fat—even when your body is resting!

Aaaaaaand...Exhale

Air and Water

When you exhale, you breathe out not only carbon dioxide, but also water! A person at rest exhales more than ½ ounce of water per hour. While that may seem like a lot, you lose about four times as much water when you exercise.

Room to Breathe

The **diaphragm** is a dome-shaped **muscle** beneath the lungs.

As you **inhale,** your diaphragm **contracts** and moves down while your intercostal muscles move your ribs **up** and **outward**, allowing space for your lungs to fill up with air like balloons.

Mouth Breathing

Breathing through your mouth increases your chances of developing a lisp. If you breathe through your mouth for a long period of time, your jaw can shrink, which can cause crooked teeth.

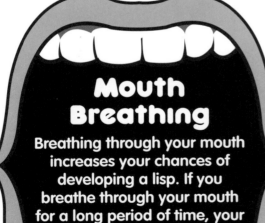

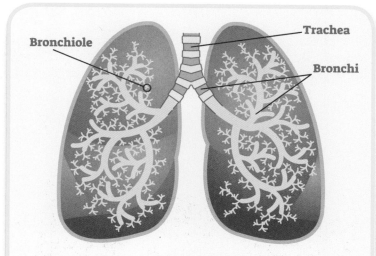

AIR TRAVEL

When you breathe in, air travels down your trachea, also known as your windpipe. Inside the trachea, tiny hairs called cilia keep dirt and mucus out of your lungs. The air then moves through a number of branches in your lungs, called the bronchi and bronchioles.

Bronchiole **Trachea** **Bronchi**

Full of Air

The average person inhales about 11,000 liters of air every day—that's enough air to fill at least 70 bathtubs!

Women and children breathe faster than men.

FUN FACTS about Pregnancy and Birth

THE LONGEST PREGNANCY ON RECORD WAS 12½ MONTHS.

The egg is the largest single cell in the female human body. It can be seen with the naked eye.

Babies cannot see COLORS when they are born. They can only see BLACK and WHITE.

34

Cheese!

ABOUT 1 iN EVERY 2,000 BABiES ARE BORN WiTH TEETH.

Most Caucasian babies are born with blue eyes. However, because of an increase in melanin, or pigment, as they get older, their eyes may continue to change color until age two.

Babies are born with kneecaps made of cartilage instead of bone. Within a few years, the cartilage hardens to bone.

Most females are capable of giving birth to **35** children in a lifetime.

Skin-teresting

SKIN

is the body's biggest organ. It has three layers: the epidermis, dermis, and subcutis.

On the Outside

The epidermis is the outermost layer of your skin and is thicker on the palms of your hands and soles of your feet than on the rest of your body. In addition to providing protection for the body, the epidermis makes melanin, which gives skin its pigment or color.

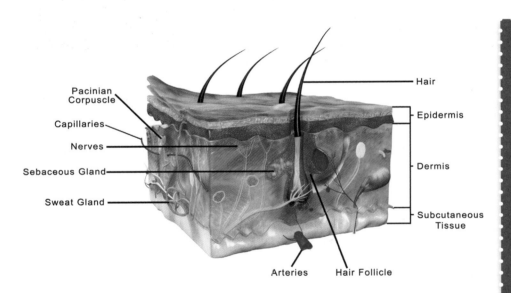

Pacinian Corpuscle

Capillaries

Nerves

Sebaceous Gland

Sweat Gland

Hair

Epidermis

Dermis

Subcutaneous Tissue

Arteries

Hair Follicle

Smack-dab in the Middle

The dermis is the middle layer of your skin. It does everything from making sweat and growing hair to helping you feel things, thanks to nerve endings that send signals to your brain to tell you if something feels soft or itchy or painful.

EVERY SQUARE INCH OF SKIN ON THE HUMAN BODY HAS ABOUT 32 MILLION BACTERIA ON IT, BUT MOST OF THEM ARE HARMLESS.

GOING DEEP

The deepest layer of your skin is the subcutis. Subcutaneous tissue connects the dermis to your muscles and bones, controls your body temperature, and stores your fat. This fat protects your muscles and bones from injury.

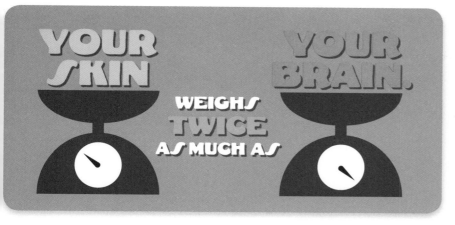

YOUR SKIN **YOUR BRAIN.** WEIGHS TWICE AS MUCH AS

Most of the dust found in your house is dead skin that has been shed.

Oily Situation

The skin has two kinds of oil glands. Sweat glands release oil, which helps cool down the skin. Sebaceous glands secrete sebum, which moisturizes your skin and prevents bacterial growth, but is also responsible for pimples and acne breakouts.

The body is constantly shedding dead skin cells, even while we are sleeping. The dead cells stay on the skin until they fall off or are brushed off, a process known as exfoliation. In one month, you will have a completely different top layer of skin than you have now.

Twins
Twice the Fun!

Twice as Nice

There are two types of twins: identical and fraternal. Identical twins happen when one sperm from the father fertilizes an egg from the mother, and the egg then splits to form two embryos. Fraternal twins develop from two different fertilized eggs, so they do not share the exact same genetics. Fraternal twins can be two boys, two girls, or one of each.

Two for One

Twins tend to be born prematurely, or early. More than 50% of twins are born before 37 weeks, weighing an average of 5 pounds, 5 ounces.

Double Up

All pregnant women have approximately the same chance of having identical twins: about 1 in 250. Some identical twins will share the same placenta and sac in the mother's womb, while others will have separate placentas and sacs. Identical twins share the same DNA but not the same fingerprints.

Spot the Difference

Twin-tastic

Find and circle 10 differences between these two pictures of sets of twins and their friends having fun in the park.

Did I Do That? Odd Things the Body Does

HICCUP!
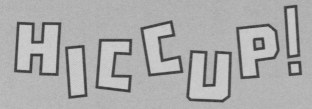

A hiccup is an involuntary spasm of the diaphragm. You can hiccup anywhere from four to 60 times per minute. Once you start hiccupping, you will usually hiccup at least 63 times before you stop. Men and women get hiccups with the same frequency, but men tend to have more persistent hiccups, which can last for more than two days.

DID YOU KNOW?

It's almost impossible to sneeze with your eyes open. Sneezing is one of your body's automatic responses.

Roll With It

About 65% to 80% of people can curl their tongues. While it is widely thought that the ability to roll your tongue is genetic, scientists have found that this is not totally accurate—it's possible for people to teach themselves how.

Your eyes stay the same size as they were on the day you were born.

WHEN THE BODY IS COLD, IT SHIVERS TO WARM UP! THIS HAPPENS BECAUSE MUSCLES CONTRACT, OR SQUEEZE TOGETHER, WHICH RELEASES ENERGY TO WARM THE BODY. SHIVERING IS AN AUTOMATIC, INVOLUNTARY RESPONSE.

HAIR-RAISING

Goose bumps, also known as the pilomotor reflex, happen when muscles attached to hair follicles tighten. They literally make your hair stand up! When you are cold, goose bumps are the body's way of trying to create insulation, or keep you warm, by trapping a layer of air against the skin. Because human hair is very thin, this isn't very effective!

FUN FACTS about Laughter

Everybody laughs! Babies as young as 17 days old can laugh.

LAUGHTER HAS THE ABILITY TO RELAX MUSCLES FOR AS LONG AS

45

MINUTES.

LAUGHTER is contagious.

Adults laugh anywhere from 15 to 30 times per day on average.

People are 30 times more likely to laugh in a group than alone.

Ten to 15 minutes of laughing can burn up to 40 calories.

Laughter raises your heart rate, blood pressure, and breathing rate.

IT'S NEARLY **IMPOSSIBLE** TO **TICKLE** YOURSELF. YOUR **BRAIN** KNOWS YOUR TOUCH FROM SOMEBODY ELSE'S.

"It takes more muscles to frown than it does to smile." This is a popular saying, but it's not quite true: Since humans tend to smile often, the muscles used to smile are stronger than the muscles we use to frown. We don't actually use more muscles to frown than to smile.

I've Got a Feeling

Express Yourself

Humans can make more than 10,000 facial expressions to show their emotions. Researchers have found that frowning can make you feel sadder and smiling can make you feel happier.

Research has shown that having a negative emotion, like depression, happens because of higher activity in the right frontal cortex of the brain. Happy emotions come from activity in the left frontal cortex.

Active Mind

WHEN YOU ARE **EMBARRASSED,** YOUR BODY **RELEASES ADRENALINE,** CAUSING YOU TO **BLUSH.** **NERVES** AT THE BASE OF YOUR **SPINE** CONTROL **BLUSHING.**

From the Heart

People used to believe that different parts of the body controlled certain moods. For example, ancient doctors thought:

HAPPINESS
came from the heart

FEAR
came from the kidneys

ANGER
came from the liver

SH[...]

Everybod[...] times—even grownups! Being shy can mean feeling nervous, uncomfortable, or timid. Shyness can cause a physical response, like blushing or shaking, and can be a result of genetics or of something that has happened to you and behaviors you have learned.

Fight or Flight

Your hands get sweaty when you're excited, anxious, or scared because of a reflex called fight-or-flight. These emotions put stress on your body, causing your body to respond as if you were in danger. Your breathing and heart rate get faster, due to hormones your body makes in response to this perceived danger.

Chew and Swallow

It Takes Two

There are two types of digestion: mechanical and chemical. Chewing is mechanical digestion, the process of physically breaking down large pieces of food into smaller pieces. Chemical digestion uses enzymes to break down these smaller bits of food into molecules that our bodies can use.

Easy to Swallow

Saliva helps you to chew and swallow by moistening your food, and it contains an enzyme that starts the chemical digestion of starchy foods. "Bolus" is the term used to describe chewed-up food right before it's swallowed.

One Direction

The epiglottis is a flap of tissue in the back of the throat that closes when you swallow to prevent food from traveling down your windpipe. While most people don't eat while upside down, they could! The muscles in the esophagus move in waves, called peristalsis, causing the food to move down instead of up. It takes approximately seven seconds for chewed food to move through the esophagus, landing in the stomach.

Digesting Food

The intestines are the organs in which the majority of digestion takes place. Help dinner move through the intestines to get from one end to the other.

START

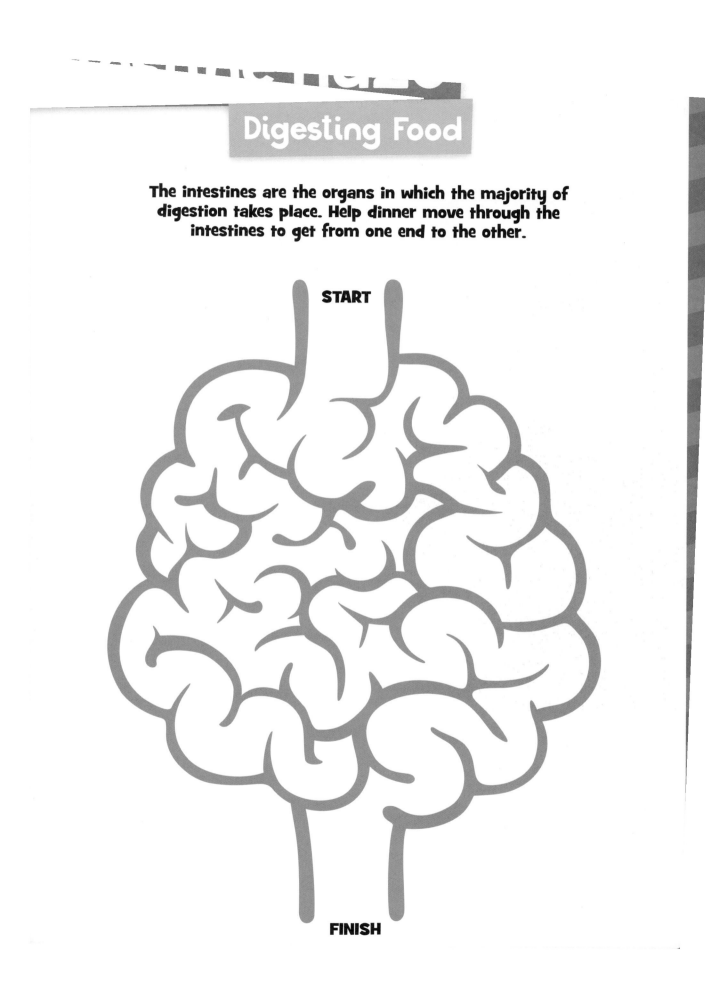

FINISH

Excuse Me! Bodily Functions

IT'S IN THE AIR

When you eat, drink, swallow, or spit, you also swallow a little air. When you digest food, gas builds up in your body and makes you burp or fart!

GOTTA GO!

Pee, also called urine, is 95% water. A person's kidneys will clean about 1 million gallons of water, turning it into pee, in a lifetime.

GARBAGE DAY, EVERY DAY

Your body acts like a trash can that is constantly filling up. You must empty it—pee and poop—every day to keep it healthy. Waste from digested food stays in your colon until it's time to get rid of it.

The **average person** goes to the **bathroom**

6 times a day.

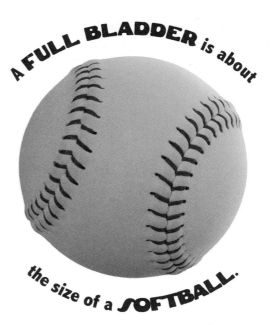

A **FULL BLADDER** is about the size of a **SOFTBALL**.

WASTE TIME

About 75% of poop is water, and the rest is germs and undigested plant fibers. Most people poop one to two times every one to two days, but everyone has his or her own schedule, due in part to the varying amounts of time it takes for a meal to move through a person's digestive system.

WHAT'S THAT SMELL?

A diet rich in sulfur—such as eggs, cabbage, milk, and onions—can cause smelly farts. The average person farts 13 to 21 times a day, releasing up to 2 liters of gas in a 24-hour period.

Tastemakers

Even though you have 9,000 of them, you can't see your taste buds—they are sensory cells that sit on top of the small bumps on your tongue, in your throat, and on the roof of your mouth. These small bumps, which you can see, are called papillae.

BITTER

SOUR

SOUR

SAVORY

SALT

SALT

SWEET

A Matter of Taste

There are five basic tastes: sweet, bitter, sour, salty, and savory. Savory is also called umami. You can sense different tastes everywhere on your tongue.

Different Tastes

Hypergeusia is a disorder that gives you an abnormally heightened sense of taste. *Hypogeusia* is a reduced sense of taste.

HAVING **NO** SENSE OF **TASTE** IS CALLED **AGEUSIA.**

YOU LOSE ABOUT HALF YOUR TASTE BUDS BY AGE 60.

Blanks

Fill in the missing letters to complete the facts below.
For help, look at the opposite page about taste.

Taste buds are __ **E** __ **S** __ __ __ cells.

Taste buds are located on your tongue, as well as in your
__ **H** __ **O** __ __ and on the roof of your __ __ **U** **T** __.

You __ **O** __ __ about half of your taste buds by age 60.

__ __ **P** __ __ **L** **A** __ are the small
bumps on which your taste buds sit.

The five basic tastes are: __ **W** __ __ __, __ __ **T** **T** __ __,
__ **O** __ __, __ __ **L** **T** __, and __ __ **V** __ __ **Y**.

Another word for "savory" is __ __ __ **M** **I**.

A reduced sense of taste is called
__ **Y** **P** __ __ **E** __ **S** __ __.

Someone with no sense of taste has __ **G** __ **U** __ __ **A**.

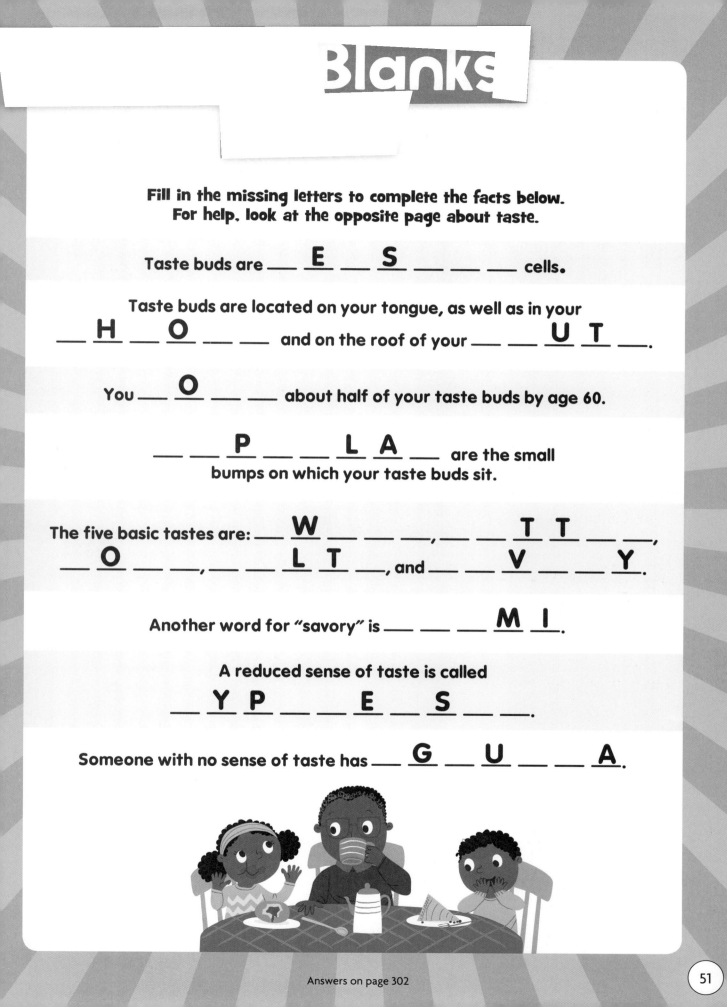

Answers on page 302

Liver

Your liver is a part of your digestive system. It sits on top of the right side of your stomach, under the diaphragm. It is the second largest organ, next to the skin. It weighs about 3 pounds and can hold ½ liter of blood!

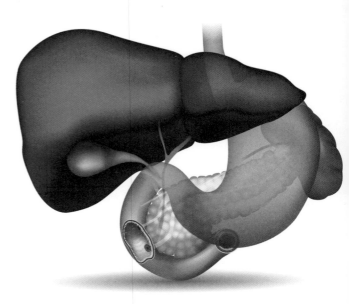

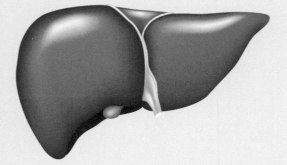

The Sum of Its Parts

Two main lobes make up the liver's cone-like shape. These lobes have eight segments each, and each segment has 1,000 lobules, or smaller lobes. The job of the lobules is to move bile to the gallbladder and small intestine.

Can't Liver Without It

Here are a few of the **over 500** functions the liver helps with:

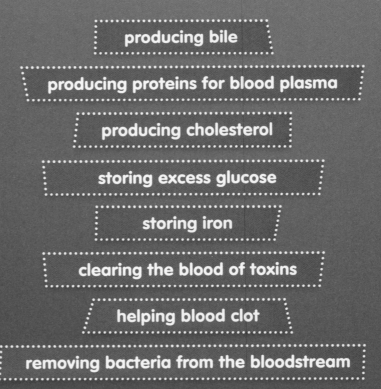

producing bile

producing proteins for blood plasma

producing cholesterol

storing excess glucose

storing iron

clearing the blood of toxins

helping blood clot

removing bacteria from the bloodstream

NEW LIVER, NEW LIFE

IN SOME CASES, A PERSON WITH **LIVER DISEASE** NEEDS A NEW LIVER AND WILL HAVE A **LIVER TRANSPLANT.** IF A DONATED LIVER COMES FROM A PERSON **WHO IS ALIVE,** THE DONOR'S LIVER CAN **REGROW ITSELF.** IN THAT CASE, BOTH PEOPLE—THE **PATIENT** AND THE **DONOR** —CAN END UP WITH HEALTHY LIVERS THAT ARE **FULLY FUNCTIONAL.**

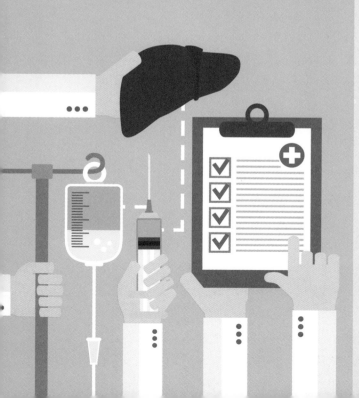

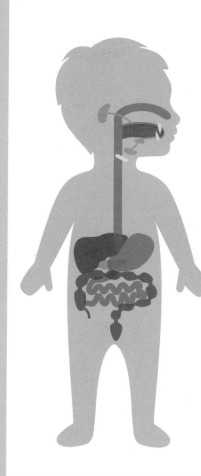

Liver It Up

The liver also helps with metabolism, or the process of turning food into energy. This organ metabolizes all carbohydrates, lipids, and proteins. In the liver, these substances are turned into other substances that are useful to the body, like glucose and cholesterol.

You Only Liver Once

It is estimated that there are more than 100 kinds of liver diseases, and some are more serious than others. Viruses, genetics, toxins, and alcohol can cause liver diseases. Some liver diseases have no known cause.

FUN FACTS about the Eyes

The **eye** is made up of many different parts, including the

cornea, iris, lens, and **retina.**

ABOUT ONE-THIRD OF THE HUMAN RACE HAS PERFECT, OR 20-20, VISION.

Most people blink about 12 times a minute. Blinking helps keep eyeballs clean and moist.

Some people are born with 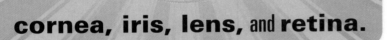 two different colored eyes.

A **BLINK** USUALLY LASTS **100** TO **150** MILLISECONDS, MEANING YOU CAN BLINK **FIVE TIMES** IN A SECOND.

THE EYE CAN DISTINGUISH ABOUT **10 MILLION** DIFFERENT COLORS.

The **MUSCLES** in your **EYES** are more **ACTIVE** than **ANY** other **MUSCLES** in your **BODY.**

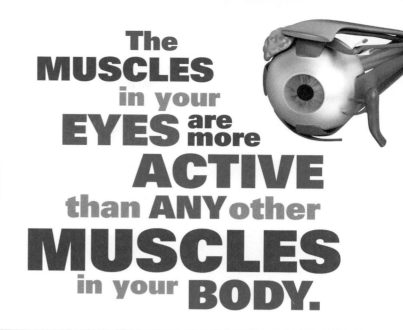

Blue-eyed people share a common ancestor with every other blue-eyed person in the world.

More people have brown eyes than any other color.

Injuries to the surface of eyes heal very fast—usually in about two to three days.

Eyebrows help keep water and sweat out of our eyes.

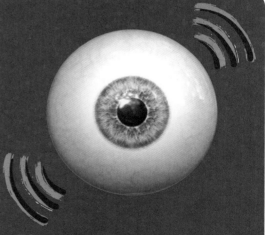

The pupils in your eyes can dilate, or become bigger, when you hear loud or unexpected noises.

55

The Nose Knows

Scents and Sensibility

Your nose can remember about 50,000 different smells! The technical term for smelling is *olfaction*. *Anosmia* is the inability to smell, and someone with a strong sense of smell is said to have *hyperosmia*. Women have stronger senses of smell than men, even though they generally have smaller noses than men.

NOTHING TO SNEEZE AT

Sneezing is more than just a simple *achoo*! When an irritant like pollen or dust gets in your nose, it is detected by the trigeminal nerve, which runs throughout your face. The irritation sets off a series of reflexes designed to get the irritant out of your body, including your throat closing and pressure building up in your lungs.

DID YOU KNOW?

YOUR SINUSES

Your nose and sinuses are closely related. Sinuses are air-filled, hollow spaces in the bones of your skull that are located in your forehead, cheeks, between your eyes, and at the back of your nose. You have 10 sinuses, which, together with your nose, produce mucus that protects your lungs. They produce almost 1 liter of mucus a day, most of which is swallowed. When you're sick, sinuses can create up to 2 liters a day.

The Great Divide

A person's nostrils are divided by the nasal septum, which is largely made up of a type of tissue called cartilage. Most nosebleeds happen in the front of the septum, because it contains tiny blood vessels that are easily damaged. Nose picking, allergies, colds, and dry, heated indoor air can cause nosebleeds.

I Smell Danger

Your brain uses your sense of smell to tell you about your environment. Your brain catalogs different smells that you have learned to associate with certain situations or things. In some cases, your sense of smell can keep you safe. For example, if you smell smoke, your brain will interpret that smell and alert you that there may be a fire.

Nature's Filter

Nose hairs are important! They help filter out dust and other debris when you breathe. Once inside your nose, air moves along grooves in the walls of your nasal cavity, where it swirls and churns like a river. Air passing through your nose is warmed to match your body temperature, or it is cooled if it is very hot, to protect your sensitive lung tissue.

Here's Looking at You, Kid!

Find Your Voice

Both boys and girls experience voice changes as they grow older. This is because your voice box, also known as your larynx, gets larger during puberty. The larynx grows larger in boys than it does in girls. In boys, puberty also causes the production of testosterone, a hormone which causes vocal cords to get longer and thicker, causing a change in the voice.

Here's the Zit-uation

Eight out of 10 teens experience acne. It commonly appears on the face, neck, chest, shoulders, and upper back. Acne in kids and teens is caused by the hormone changes of puberty. New hormones cause the oil glands in the skin to produce more sebum, or oil. Too much oil clogs pores, which leads to acne.

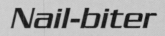

Nail-biter

Around 50% of children and teens bite their nails. It's possible that nail biting is genetic. Scientists aren't sure, but they have found that parents who bite their nails have children who are more likely to bite their nails, too. Studies show that this happens even if the parents have stopped biting their nails before they have children.

Working Heart

AS A KID, YOUR HEART IS ABOUT THE SAME SIZE AS YOUR FIST.

All the Allergies

About 3 million kids in the United States have food allergies, or negative bodily reactions to food, most commonly to nuts, seafood, milk, eggs, soy, or wheat. Some children can outgrow milk, egg, wheat, and soy allergies by the time they become adults. However, allergies to tree nuts, peanuts, and shellfish are usually lifelong.

Children generally have a better sense of smell than adults.

Sensitive Subjects

Children are more sensitive to different tastes than adults. Studies have shown that young people have a higher concentration of the type of taste buds that make them more sensitive to sweet flavors. As children age, they show a better sense of being able to recognize different flavors, and there is a decrease in their preference for sweet tastes.

THE TOOTH OF THE MATTER

Humans develop their teeth in two stages. The first set that grows in childhood is what we call baby teeth and includes a person's first 20 teeth. Baby teeth fall out starting when a person is about six years old and are replaced by a new set of 32 permanent teeth, often called adult teeth, usually by the time a person turns 12.

Teeth Underneath

Both your baby teeth and your adult teeth start to develop before you are even born! Even though a baby's teeth aren't visible at birth, the tooth buds of his or her baby teeth, as well as the adult teeth, are already present in the baby's jaw. The only exception is the wisdom teeth, which usually develop in the teenage years.

TOUGH TEETH

The outside of teeth, called enamel, is the hardest part of your body. Your gums, also called gingiva, are the pink tissue surrounding your teeth. Gums help anchor your teeth in your mouth and keep them in line.

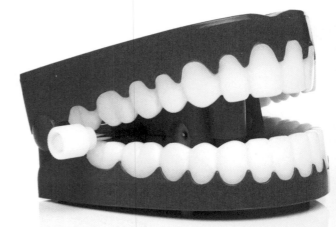

TYPES OF TEETH

There are many different kinds of teeth, including molars, premolars, canines, and incisors, each designed to perform a different function. Incisors bite food, canines tear food, and molars grind food. Wisdom teeth, or third molars, got their nickname because they come in when a person is older and wiser.

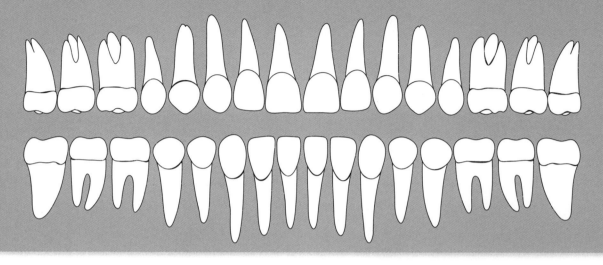

THE TOOTH IS THE ONLY PART OF THE HUMAN BODY THAT CANNOT HEAL.

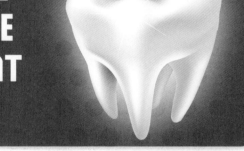

DON'T BRUSH THIS OFF

Most Americans will spend an average of 38½ days of their lives brushing their teeth. Brushing and flossing is the most effective way to remove plaque, the transparent layer of bacteria coating the teeth. Plaque causes cavities, it's important to brush and floss daily.

Working Up a Sweat

Everyone sweats when they are overheated or building up heat through exercise, and many people sweat when they are stressed, but the two types of sweat aren't the same. Regular sweat consists of water, potassium, and salt, and it cools down the body when it evaporates. Stress sweat comes from a different gland than regular sweat and is made up of fatty acids and proteins; it doesn't evaporate as fast as regular sweat.

The Wettest Sweat

Hyperhidrosis is the medical term for having overactive sweat glands, or sweating too much. It can be caused by medical conditions or medications and can lead to dehydration.

Sweat is actually **odorless**. It gets its smell from the **bacteria** that live in your skin.

Who's the Better Sweater?

A body has between 2 and 5 million sweat glands. Even though women have more sweat glands than men, men tend to produce more sweat than women.

Crossword Puzzle

Exercise

Complete the crossword using the clues below.
For help, look at the pages about exercise.

ACROSS

2. Having fun, like at the playground

5. Chemicals released by the body during exercise

7. Moving faster than walking

9. Moving your body, usually for better health

11. Human tissue that works together to produce movement

12. Part of the body where sweat is made and released

DOWN

1. People who can touch their toes are said to have this

3. The ability to perform a movement, like exercise, for a long period of time

4. A form of exercise that uses different ways of breathing and movement, or poses

6. Having this allows you to lift heavy objects

8. To extend your arms and legs

10. Another name for perspiration

Answers on page 303

Sweet Dreams

The Science of Sleep and Dreaming

HUMANS SPEND ONE-THIRD OF THEIR LIVES SLEEPING.

I've Got Rhythm

Tick, tock—you have a biological clock! Known as circadian rhythm, this is your brain's way of regulating how long you sleep and how long you are awake during a 24-hour period. Staying up too late or sleeping in too long can throw off this rhythm. When a person has trouble falling asleep or staying asleep, he or she is experiencing insomnia, the most common sleep disorder. Approximately 10% to 15% of adults have insomnia.

You can go without eating for weeks, but 11 days is tops for going without sleep.

REM-ember that Dream?

Most dreams are forgotten minutes after waking, though people who daydream are more likely to remember their nighttime dreams. If you wake up during REM sleep, you are more likely to remember your dream than if you wake up after a full night of sleep.

Dream On

We have most of our vivid, or clear and lifelike, dreams during REM sleep, because that is when the brain is most active. Dreams may last anywhere from five to 45 minutes, and most people have about four dreams every night. That adds up to about 1,460 dreams a year!

ALL THE SLEEP'S A STAGE

There are five stages of sleep, and we repeat them every 90 minutes while we are asleep. Stage 1 sleep is marked by a slower breathing rate and is considered light sleep. Stage 1 sleep is short—after about two minutes you enter into stage 2 sleep.

For the 20 minutes of stage 2 sleep, your body temperature lowers and your breathing becomes regular.

If you sleepwalk or talk in your sleep, you most likely are in stage 3 or 4 of sleep. These stages are deep and restorative, helping the body feel renewed, and together they last about 30 minutes.

The fifth and final stage is called REM (rapid eye movement) sleep. Completing all five stages is considered a cycle. You typically go through four or five cycles before waking up.

A cool room may help you **SLEEP** better.

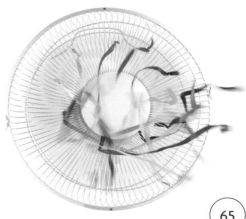

Give Me a Hand

In Good Hands

Each hand has two main sets of muscles and tendons that work to make it move. Flexor muscles connect to the underside of the forearm and bend the fingers and thumb. Extensors connect to the top of the forearm and straighten the fingers and thumb.

There is no hair on your palms.

Hand-to-Hand

An average adult woman's hand is 6.7 inches long. The average length for a man's hand is 7.4 inches.

When typing, the average person use the LEFT hand more than *the RIGHT*.

Talk to the Hand

Hands can be used to speak. American Sign Language (ASL) is a complete language that uses signs made by moving the hands to communicate. ASL is used by many people in North America who are deaf or have trouble hearing.

Put a Ring On It

The third finger is known as the ring finger. Women and men will sometimes wear rings on their left ring fingers to show that they are married or engaged.

Feeling Left Out?

About 10% of people are left-handed—or "lefties." Nobody knows why some people use their left hands instead of their right to do everything from eating to writing, but scientists think it is at least partly genetic. Lefties tend to have more left-handed family members, and researchers have seen different brain wiring between righties and lefties.

There are EIGHT bones in the wrist.

THERE ARE 27 BONES IN THE HAND.

There are five bones in the palm, which connect to your four fingers and thumb.

It's In Your Blood

BLOOD TYPES

All blood is made of the same basic elements, but not all blood is identical.

The most common blood type is O positive.

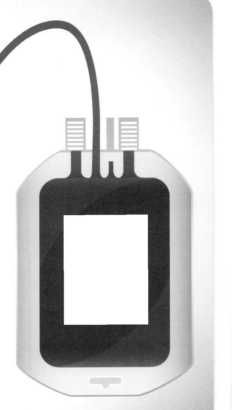

Flesh and Blood

After red blood cells develop in bone marrow, they circulate through the body for about 120 days.

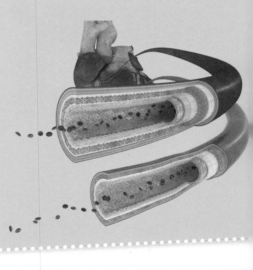

DID YOU KNOW?

Bone marrow is the tissue in the middle of large bones, and it is a bit like a **THICK JELLY**. Bone marrow makes blood cells.

A kitchen faucet would have to be turned on all the way and run for at least 45 years to equal the amount of blood pumped in an average lifetime.

Blood
PUMPS
through
the
AORTA
at
ONE
mile per hour.

SPEED LIMIT 1

BLOOD CELLS BY THE BILLION

There are 150 billion red blood cells in 1 ounce of blood, and white blood cells make up about 1% of blood. Red blood cells move through your entire body in about 20 seconds.

Around the World

Healthy Food from Across the Globe

Curry Favor

In Malaysia, a spice called turmeric is used to make curry and is loved for its taste and antioxidant properties. Turmeric contains curcumin, which can lessen inflammation and might help with problems like arthritis. Curcumin might even help slow down tumors as they grow.

Kola-borate and Listen

Kola nuts grow in Africa. People chew them before they eat—it is thought that this helps digest food. The nuts are tasteless and contain caffeine. They can increase the oxygen in blood and have even been shown to slow the spread of the bacteria that causes illnesses like tuberculosis.

Cuckoo for Coconuts

In Thailand, the coconut—specifically coconut milk—has long been considered a health food. Coconut milk and coconut water are rich in vitamins B12 and D, as well as electrolytes, which help to hydrate the body. They also provide plenty of calcium.

Word Scramble

Global Foods

Unscramble the letters to find words about healthy things for your body, healthy food from other places, and where to find them. For help, look at the opposite page.

MAVSTINI

_ _ _ _ _ _ _ _

OUNCCOT

_ _ _ _ _ _ _

CTMUERRI

_ _ _ _ _ _ _ _

OAKL

_ _ _ _

MURICCNU

_ _ _ _ _ _ _ _

DAYRTHE

_ _ _ _ _ _ _

SALIMAYA

_ _ _ _ _ _ _ _

AULMCIC

_ _ _ _ _ _ _

ADITALHN

_ _ _ _ _ _ _ _

CRAIFA

_ _ _ _ _ _

ROLSTETLECEY

_ _ _ _ _ _ _ _ _ _ _ _

FUN FACTS about
Babies

A baby's head makes up 25% of his or her body weight.

On average, babies start smiling at about 12 weeks of age.

INFANTS only BLINK about ONCE a MINUTE.

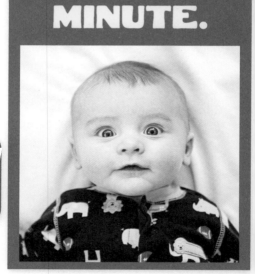

Until about seven months old, babies can breathe and swallow at the same time.

Babies dream a lot! About 80% of newborn sleep time and up to 50% of a baby's sleep time after the first month is REM sleep, when most dreaming happens.

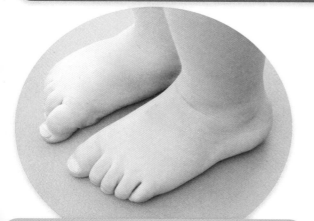

A baby's feet don't have arches. Arches usually appear on most children when they are around two years old. Some people never develop arches and have flat feet.

A newborn **BABY** only has about one cup of blood in his or her body.

Human babies aren't the only mammals that smile in their sleep—newborn chimpanzees and monkeys do, too!

BABIES CAN'T TASTE SALT UNTIL THEY ARE BETWEEN TWO AND SIX MONTHS OLD.

NEWBORNS MAKE NOISE TO CRY, BUT THEY DON'T SHED ANY TEARS. TEARS AREN'T MADE UNTIL BABIES ARE ONE TO THREE MONTHS OLD.

Walk It Off

Walk the Walk

If you walk between 8,000 and 10,000 steps a day, you will end up walking about 115,000 miles in your lifetime. That's like walking around the world four times!

Toe Long

According to research, about 20% to 30% of people have a second toe that is longer than the first.

DID YOU KNOW?

There are 26 bones in a foot and nearly 8,000 nerves.

YOUR **FOREARM** (FROM THE INSIDE OF YOUR ELBOW TO THE INSIDE OF YOUR WRIST) IS THE SAME LENGTH AS YOUR FOOT.

Trans-foot-mation

Your foot size can continue to change, even as an adult. As you get older, the tendons and ligaments that hold the bones together in the foot lose elasticity, or the ability to stretch and spring back into place, making your feet longer and wider.

A Feat for Feet

Feet grow quickly during the first year of a child's life—his or her feet will be nearly half their adult size by the end of that year. By the time a child is 12, his or her feet will be about 90% of their adult size.

What Are Your Digits?

Here's a Finger Tip

Fingertips can send messages to the brain through highly sensitive receptors, making your fingers even more sensitive than your eyes. Some scientists think that our fingerprints may improve our sense of touch, while others believe they help wick water off our fingertips. Other researchers believe our fingerprints allow skin to stretch more easily to prevent things like blisters and protect from damage.

The nail on your middle finger grows faster than the nails on your other fingers.

Fingernails grow faster than toenails.

If you lose a fingernail, it will take about six months to grow a new one because fingernails grow about $1/10$ inch each month.

In the Palm of Your Hand

There are 34 muscles in the palms and forearms that make the fingers work. When one of these muscles contracts, it pulls on a tendon in your finger, which then tugs on the bone and moves it.

Don't Catch This

The medical name for toenail fungus is *onychomycosis*. If you have a toenail fungus, it doesn't mean that you have an infection throughout your body—toenail fungus usually stays on the nail itself or on the nail bed, the area surrounding the nail. However, it is contagious and can be easily picked up in places like a public pool or gym locker room if you don't wear shoes or socks!

NO TWO PEOPLE HAVE THE SAME FINGERPRINTS. BESIDES PEOPLE, KOALAS, CHIMPANZEES, AND GORILLAS ARE THE ONLY OTHER LIVING CREATURES THAT HAVE FINGERPRINTS.

Two Thumbs Up, Down, and Around

Humans are not the only primates possessing opposable thumbs—thumbs that can rotate independently and move toward the fingers. Other primates, like gorillas, chimpanzees, orangutans, baboons, Colobus monkeys, and gibbons, also have opposable thumbs. Humans can move their thumbs farther across their hands than any other primate, though!

Can You Hear Me Now?

Listen to This

Even though your ears detect sound, your brain does most of the work of listening—ears turn sound waves into nerve impulses that are then sent to the brain. It's the brain's job to understand and make sense of the noise delivered by the ears.

What You Need to Hear

Deep in the inner ear is the cochlea, which is spiral shaped and helps with hearing. The inner ear also contains microscopic hair cells that respond to sound waves, which then travel to the brain as nerve impulses.

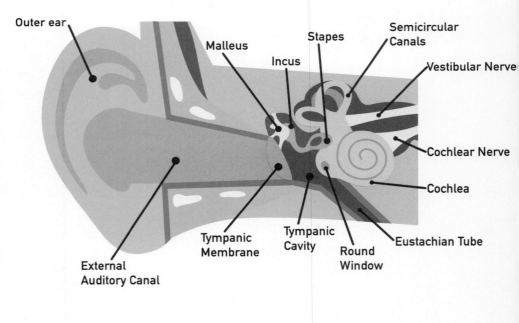

Outer ear · Malleus · Incus · Stapes · Semicircular Canals · Vestibular Nerve · Cochlear Nerve · Cochlea · Eustachian Tube · Round Window · Tympanic Cavity · Tympanic Membrane · External Auditory Canal

Small but Not Ear-relevant

The stirrup bone, or stapes, works together with the malleus, and incus bones—also known as the hammer and anvil, respectively—to help sound travel from the eardrum to the inner ear.

WAX FACTS

The wax in your ears isn't actually wax! While it feels and looks like wax, it's really just a mixture of oil, sweat, dead skin cells, hair, and dirt that prevents dust—and even small bugs—from getting inside. There are two types of earwax: Some people have dry earwax that is flaky and gray in color, while other people have wet, yellowish-brown earwax. Your genetics determine which type of earwax you have.

Eeeew!

Ear-itation

The area of the ear behind the eardrum contains the Eustachian tube, which balances pressure and drains mucus. Ear infections happen when fluid behind the eardrum doesn't properly drain and becomes infected. Because kids have smaller Eustachian tubes and their immune systems are still developing, they are more prone to developing ear infections.

LET'S POP THE QUESTION

Why do your ears pop when you're on a plane? Pressure changes on planes, especially during takeoff and landing. On a plane, it's harder for the Eustachian tube to keep up with those changes to equalize pressure, so you get a blocked feeling. Swallowing, yawning, and chewing can help push air into the Eustachian tube to pop your ears and balance pressure.

Coughs, Colds, and Germs

Having a **FEVER** is a good thing—it's your body's way of fighting off **SICKNESS.**

Not all **GERMS** are bad. There are **BACTERIA** in your stomach that help you **DIGEST** food, and bacteria on your skin that allow blood to **CLOT** when you are cut.

You Have to C It to Believe It

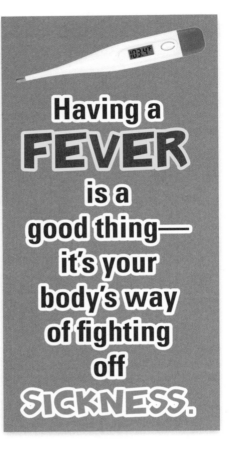

Kids and grownups get about seven colds per year. Taking vitamin C won't really help you avoid the common cold—if you have 0.2 grams or more of vitamin C a day, you won't have fewer colds, but the ones you do get may not last quite as long. The best way to prevent getting sick is to wash your hands!

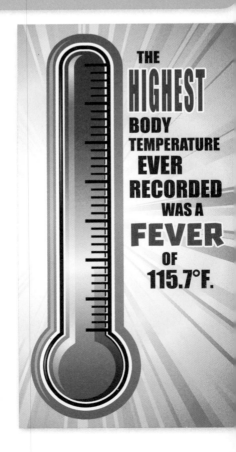

THE **HIGHEST** BODY TEMPERATURE EVER RECORDED WAS A **FEVER** OF **115.7°F.**

Snot a Joke

Snot is made of water as well as tiny particles that are in the air we breathe, like germs, dust, and pollen. When all that dries out, it turns into a booger.

Don't Chicken Out

Chickens don't cause **CHICKEN POX;** a virus causes chicken pox. It usually is a mild disease that causes small red, itchy spots. Chicken pox is less common today than it was in the past because most children are vaccinated against this virus.

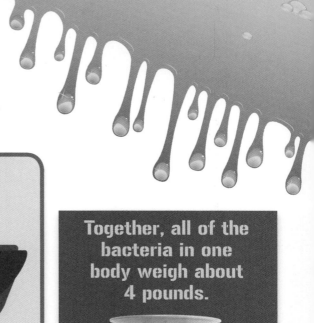

Together, all of the bacteria in one body weigh about 4 pounds.

COUGHING CAN CAUSE AIR TO MOVE **THROUGH** YOUR WINDPIPE *FASTER THAN THE SPEED OF SOUND* — OVER **1,000** FEET PER SECOND!

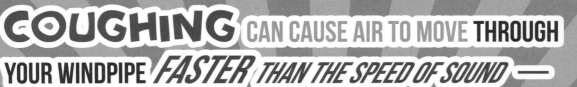

ONCE YOU EXPEL THE COUGH, THE DROPLETS THAT CONTAIN THE VIRUS CAN TRAVEL UP TO 6 FEET. NEXT TIME YOU'RE AROUND SOMEONE WHO IS SICK, YOU MIGHT WANT TO LEAVE MORE THAN 6 FEET BETWEEN YOU TWO!

Systems of the Body
Skeletal System

Stand Up Straight

The skeletal system is comprised of the axial skeleton and the appendicular skeleton. Your vertebrae, rib cage, and skull make up your axial skeleton. You can stand upright in part because of your axial skeleton; it transfers weight from your head and the top part of your body to the lower part of your body.

Run with It

The 126 bones of the appendicular skeleton help with running and walking, and they protect the organs of the digestive, excretory, and reproductive systems. The appendicular skeleton includes the bones of your upper and lower limbs, or your arms and your legs.

IT'S IN OUR BONES

Male and female skeletons are different because women can have babies and men can't! A female pelvis, which is a key component of child bearing, is more rounded and flatter than a male pelvis, and it is also larger in proportion to a woman's body.

Male   Female

A GROWING BODY

Males grow until they are in their late teens. Females stop growing about two years after they begin their menstrual cycles. Bones stop growing when the growth plates close.

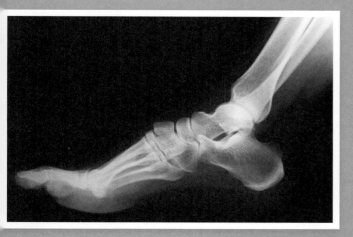

To the Bone

Bones can get diseases, just like the rest of your body. Doctors use X-rays, MRIs, and bone density tests to diagnose bone issues. Some of the more common skeletal issues are osteoporosis, arthritis, and scoliosis.

CATCHING A BREAK

Even though bones are strong and protective, they can break. In fact, breaks, strains, and fractures are common. It only takes about 10 to 15 pounds of pressure to break a bone, but bones like the skull and the femur, or thighbone, can handle more pressure and are harder to break.

FUN FACTS about the Human Body

THE SMELL OF...
INCREAS...
WAVES THAT...

THE GAP BETWEEN YOUR NOSE AND UPPER LIP IS CALLED THE PHILTRUM.

In the span of 24 hours, you will take about 23,000 breaths.

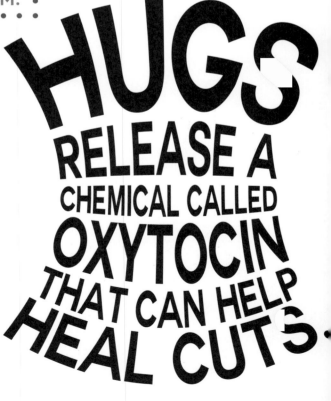

HUGS RELEASE A CHEMICAL CALLED OXYTOCIN THAT CAN HELP HEAL CUTS.

HAIR AND NAILS ARE MADE OF THE SAME PROTEIN CALLED KERATIN.

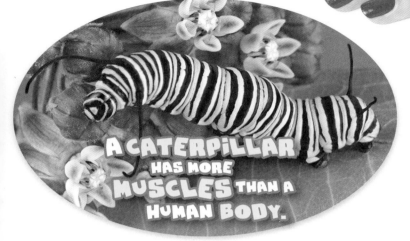

A CATERPILLAR HAS MORE MUSCLES THAN A HUMAN BODY.

EATING TOO MANY CARROTS CAN CAUSE YOUR SKIN TO TURN ORANGE.

We have 50% of the same DNA as a *banana.*

speed of a sneeze is about 100 miles per hour. Cheetahs, the fastest land ... can run at only 60 miles per hour!

The color of
your skin, eyes,
and hair depends
on the amount
of the chemical
called melanin
that you produce.

ONE IN A MELANIN

Melanin is a dark brown or black
pigment made in the epidermis layer
of your skin. Not everyone makes the
same amount of melanin, though all humans
have about the same number of melanin-making
cells. The more melanin your skin produces,
the darker your skin will be.

Sunny Vitamin

Vitamin D is very important. It helps bodies absorb calcium needed for bones to grow, among other benefits. Your body can make vitamin D by itself but only after your skin has been exposed to the sun. Sunscreen, which helps protect your skin from the sun's harmful UV rays, won't stop your body from making vitamin D.

Rising With the Sun

Sun causes your body to make more melanin. Melanin helps protect your skin from sun damage such as suntans and sunburn by deflecting or absorbing the sun's harmful rays. However, melanin alone isn't strong enough to protect your skin. You should always wear sunscreen!

An albino person has little to no pigment, or color, in his or her skin, eyes, and hair. Approximately 1 in 17,000 people are born albinos.

There are two kinds of freckles: *ephelides* and *lentigines.* Ephelides are flat, light brown, and can get darker or fade depending on time spent in the sunshine. They get darker when you're out in the sun for long periods of time, which is why they are often more noticeable in the summer months. Lentigines, also known as age spots (seen at right), typically don't change with sun exposure.

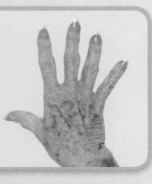

My, How You've Grown

SPURT IT OUT

Kids gain pounds and inches in short bursts known as growth spurts. How long a growth spurt lasts and how much you grow during one of them varies from person to person. Nobody knows why you might have a growth spurt one month but not the next, but it does seem to be linked to the seasons—kids grow faster in the spring!

BEARD NECESSITIES

Facial hair grows faster than any other body hair. If a man didn't trim or shave his beard, it could **GROW** to be over **30** feet long!

ONCE WE REACH OUR PEAK HEIGHT, WE START TO GRADUALLY SHRINK FROM THE TIME WE'RE 30 YEARS OLD ON.

BONE-AFIDE GROWTH

A baby's skeleton has around 300 bones. Most of these bones are made of cartilage and turn into bone over time in a process called ossification.

Adults have fewer bones than babies because, as babies grow, their bones grow together. Cartilage stops converting to bone around the end of puberty—when that happens, you stop getting taller.

THE AVERAGE HEIGHT OF AN ADULT HUMAN IS ABOUT 5 TO 6 FEET TALL.

If you NEVER cut your hair, it could GROW up to 5 feet long!

GETTING FREQUENT TRIMS DOES NOT MAKE YOUR HAIR GROW FASTER.

Top of the Morning

You are TALLER in the MORNING than at NIGHT. This may be because gravity compresses your spine, or pushes it together, as you stand up, sit down, and move around in the daytime. When you are lying down, the spine decompresses, or stretches out, so you may be taller after lying in bed all night.

Stomach Myths

MYTH: SHRINKING STOMACH

If you eat less, your stomach won't shrink. By eating less, you might be able to reset your "full meter," so you might not feel as hungry as you normally would after consistently eating less; but once you are an adult, your stomach stays essentially the same size.

Myth: CRUNCHING Your Stomach Small

Sit-ups and crunches won't make your stomach smaller. Exercise can't change the size of the actual stomach organ, but it can help lessen the layers of fat over your stomach. Exercise also can firm up the muscles of your abdomen.

Myth: Sizing UP Your Stomach with Weight

How much you weigh isn't an indicator of the size of your stomach. Thin people can have the same size stomachs—or even larger stomachs—than people who are overweight.

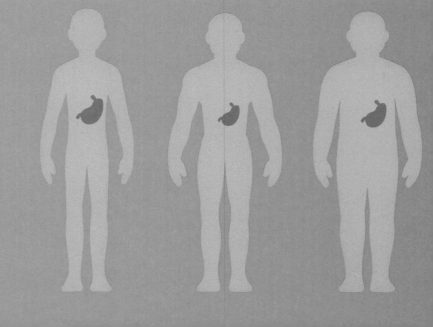

Word Search
Systems of the Body

Look at the puzzle below and see if you can find these words all about the digestive and lymphatic systems. Circle the words going across, up and down, and diagonally. Some words may be backwards!

ABSORB	GALLBLADDER	LYMPHATIC
BILE	ILEUM	NODES
CHYME	INTESTINE	SPLEEN
DIGEST	JEJUNUM	STOMACH
DUODENUM	LIVER	WASTE

```
S E D O N D N D Q K L C D O N
C K Z O B C U C A N I I K M D
I P P S E O N N O E V B W T W
F N R H D Z S T M L E X U A W
J E T E K B B Y K Y R J S M O
R M N E R O H V W M B T G H Y
T U U O S C Q U V P E I W H G
M D S N J T T B S H L N X I
E B H A U E I H C A M O T S H
A D P I Y J N N G T M T N F H
C N S P L E E N E I L S P M J
L N V A V E X J T C V E C B L
K I F T T V U H G G O G L A E
F X S B G V P M H A G I K I D
G A L L B L A D D E R D S U B
```

Think About It

Your brain controls everything you do. It's like your own personal computer.

Unlike a computer, however, there is no limit to how much you can learn. Your brain storage can never be full!

The **RIGHT SIDE** of your **BRAIN** tells the **LEFT SIDE** of your **BODY** what to do,

Zzzz

Your brain works hard at night! There is more activity in the brain while we sleep than when we are awake, thanks to the different types of brain waves the brain uses. During the day, the brain uses alpha and beta waves, but at night when we're asleep, the brain uses theta waves, which have a greater amplitude, or volume, than daytime waves.

and the **LEFT SIDE** of your **BRAIN** controls the **RIGHT SIDE** of your **BODY.**

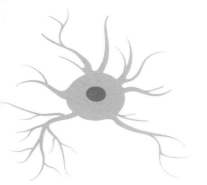

Making Waves

As the brain is working, it creates electric fields made up of neurons. When you're taking it easy, a bunch of neurons get together and form a larger electric field. When you're busy, neurons arrange themselves in more complicated patterns.

HIGH MAINTENANCE

The brain needs a lot of support to perform its daily functions! The brain uses about 20% of the body's total oxygen, even though it makes up just about 2% of a person's total body weight. It also receives about 30% of the blood being pumped by the heart.

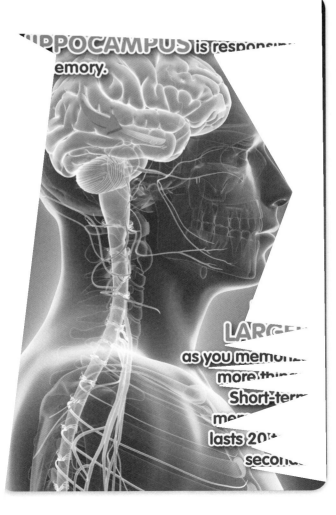

HIPPOCAMPUS is responsi...
...emory.

LARGE...
as you memori...
more thin...
Short-term
me...
lasts 20...
secon...

MEN USE THE LEFT SIDE OF THEIR BRAINS TO LISTEN, BUT WOMEN USE BOTH SIDES.

Circulatory System

All Systems Go

Sometimes the circulatory system is called the cardiovascular system. This system is more than simply a way for the blood to travel around the body; it's actually the name for three systems working together: the cardiovascular system, which involves the heart; the pulmonary system, involving the lungs; and the systemic system, made up of vessels, veins, and arteries.

DID YOU KNOW?

One of the leading causes of death in the United States is cardiovascular disease, which is a disease of the circulatory system.

Your Best Interests at Heart

Doctors who diagnose and treat circulatory issues are called cardiologists. Cardiologists are doctors of internal medicine who study the heart, veins, and arteries, and can further specialize in specific areas, such as transplant surgeries.

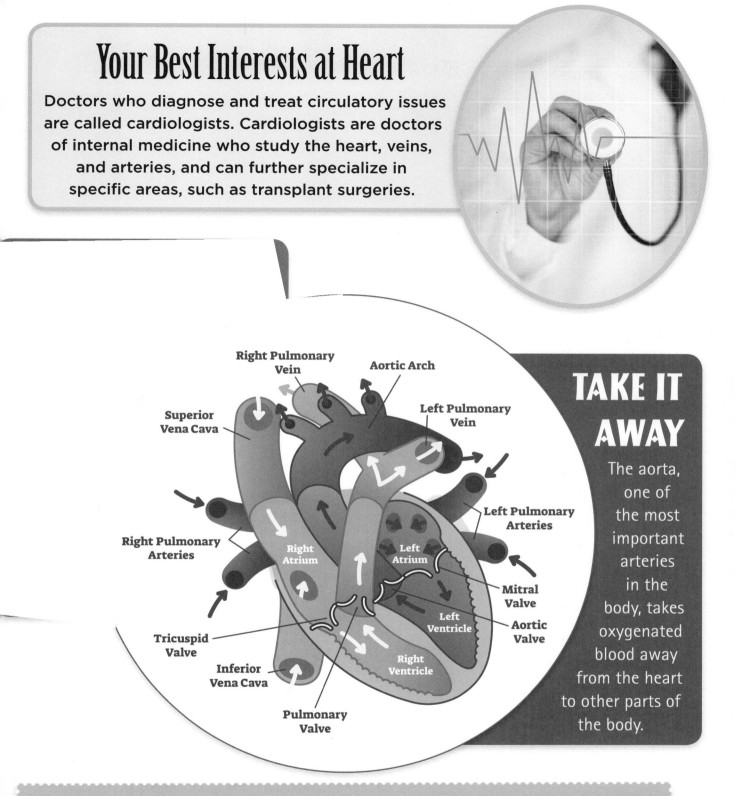

Right Pulmonary Vein

Aortic Arch

Left Pulmonary Vein

Superior Vena Cava

Right Pulmonary Arteries

Left Pulmonary Arteries

Right Atrium

Left Atrium

Mitral Valve

Aortic Valve

Left Ventricle

Tricuspid Valve

Inferior Vena Cava

Right Ventricle

Pulmonary Valve

TAKE IT AWAY

The aorta, one of the most important arteries in the body, takes oxygenated blood away from the heart to other parts of the body.

CHAMBERS OF SECRETS

When the heart pumps, blood lacking oxygen comes into the heart through the right atrium, which is one of the heart's four chambers. Valves in the heart open and close to allow blood to flow through the heart and arteries and, eventually, to the lungs. There, the blood absorbs fresh oxygen and begins its journey through the body and back to the heart.

Navel Gazing

IN 'N' OUT

If your belly button goes inward, you have an "innie." If your belly button protrudes out, you have an "outie." The shape of a person's belly button depends on many things, including how the belly button scar attaches to the muscle under it, how loose the skin around the belly button is, and the amount of fat under the skin.

Scarred for Life

Belly buttons, or navels, are actually scars from when your umbilical cord was cut. The umbilical cord is an unborn baby's connection to its mother. The unborn baby, or fetus, gets food and oxygen through the cord until he or she is born. A baby's cord is cut immediately after birth, leaving only a belly button.

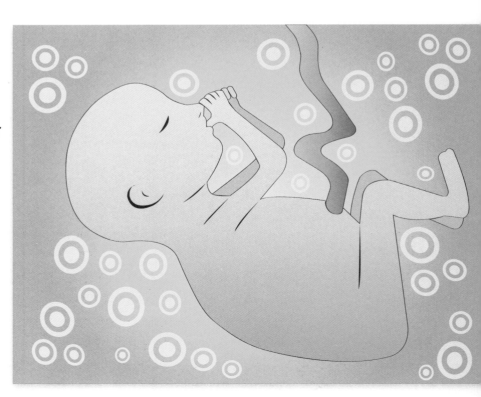

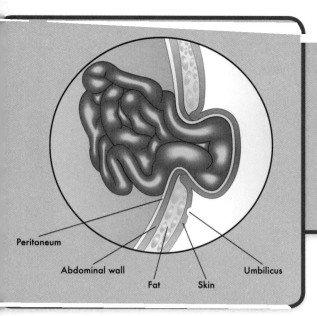

Peritoneum

Abdominal wall

Fat Skin

Umbilicus

WEAK SPOT

When intestine, fluid, or fat pushes through a weak spot in the stomach, it causes an umbilical hernia. An umbilical hernia creates a bulge near the belly button. These types of hernias often occur in infants, but most of the time they close on their own within the first year of a baby's life.

MOST **BELLY BUTTONS** BEGIN AS **OUTIES,** BUT THE MAJORITY WILL **SINK IN** TO BECOME **INNIES.**

ONLY ABOUT 10% OF HUMANS HAVE OUTIES.

DID YOU KNOW?

The bacteria in your belly button are unique to you! In addition to bacteria, scientists have found clothing fibers, hair, and dead skin cells in people's belly buttons. Make sure you wash your belly button when you take a shower or a bath.

Pushing Buttons

When a woman is pregnant, her belly button shape can change. The growth of her stomach can cause an innie belly button to pop out and become an outie, even though the belly button itself doesn't really change. After the baby is born, the belly button often goes back to its original shape.

Food for Thought

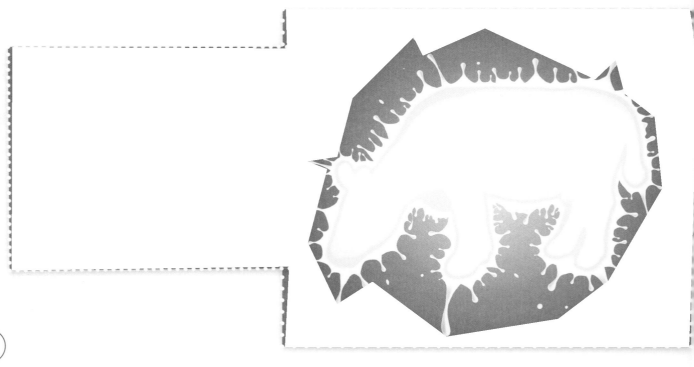

You Are What You Eat

The type of food you eat can affect how you feel afterward. Foods that are high in processed, or man-made, sugar are digested quickly so you feel hungry again soon after, while foods high in protein and fats are digested much more slowly, so you can go longer before feeling hungry again.

Food Safety

The Centers for Disease Control and Prevention (CDC) reports that around 48 million people get sick from food poisoning each year. In some cases, food poisoning can be fatal. To prevent food poisoning, store food carefully in a temperature-controlled environment and prepare food properly to avoid potentially dangerous bacteria and viruses that can live in food.

Tr-eat Yourself Right

Healthy food helps your body work right—like gas makes a car go. Eating too much sugar messes with the signals that your brain sends to tell your stomach it's full, while eating natural food helps make you smarter and improves your grades at school.

Water You Drinking?

You should drink 2 liters or about ½ gallon of water per day. On average, we drink about 16,000 gallons of water in a lifetime.

Search & Find®

Doctor's Office

It's not only important to see the doctor when you are sick—but also when you are healthy for a well-check visit, or checkup. At a well-check visit, the doctor will make sure that you are developing and will check things like your heartbeat, temperature, and blood pressure.

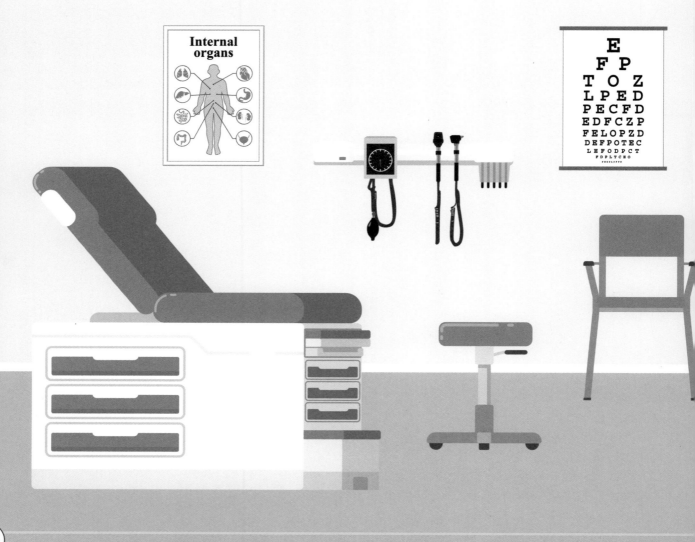

Search & Find® these items at the doctor's office:

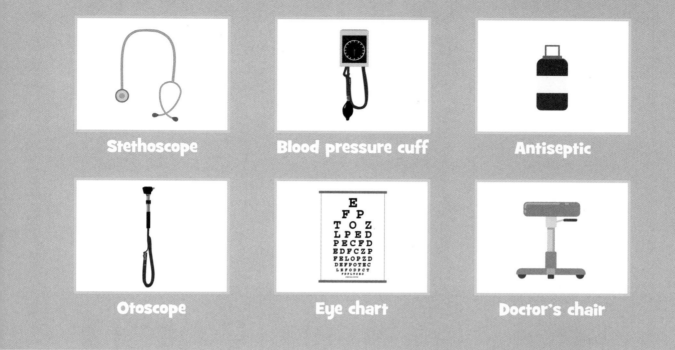

Stethoscope

Blood pressure cuff

Antiseptic

Otoscope

Eye chart

Doctor's chair

Answers on page 306

Artificial Body Parts

BIONIC BODIES

The word "bionic" is used to describe artificial limbs, because bionics is the study of how electric systems are designed to imitate or work with organic, natural systems to help solve problems. "Bionic" is also used to refer to superhuman abilities, thanks to TV shows featuring characters with bionic implants, like *The Six Million Dollar Man*.

A New Heart

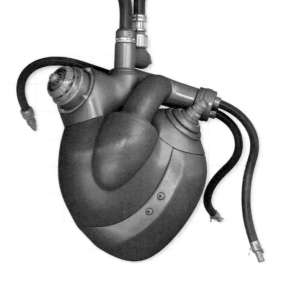

The first partial artificial heart was implanted in 1966. What was considered the first successful human heart transplant happened in 1967, though the patient died a few weeks later. The first total artificial heart was implanted in 1969, which allowed the patient to survive until a heart donor arrived three days later. Scientists have since invented artificial hearts that not only create a pulse but also maintain blood flow.

No More Bad Blood

The first artificial kidney was invented by Dr. Willem Kolff. He made a machine using sausage casings, a drum, salt water, a special pump, a motor, and orange juice cans! His invention led to modern dialysis, the process that lets a machine clean and filter the blood of people whose real kidneys have failed.

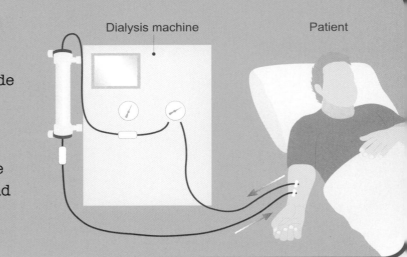

Dialysis machine   Patient

NO SKIN OFF YOUR BACK!

Experiments in growing organs and body parts in the lab still have a long way to go, but in fall 2015, Italian doctor Michele De Luca successfully transplanted healthy lab-grown skin onto the entire body of a boy suffering from a skin disease. The lab-grown skin was made by taking some of the boy's own skin, fixing the genetic defect in it that led to the disease, and growing new skin. The new skin works just like everyone else's, and grows and changes with the patient.

An Egyptian Prescription

The oldest recorded artificial body part was discovered in Cairo, Egypt: a prosthetic toe made of leather and wood that was found attached to the remains of a nearly 3,000-year-old Egyptian woman.

Out on a Limb

While a relatively new procedure, doctors are experimenting with transplanting, or transferring, limbs. There has been some success, as several patients have received hand transplants.

Any Stretch of the Imagination

Stretching has many benefits! It increases blood flow and oxygen levels and helps carry important nutrients to your muscles. Stretching also removes metabolic waste, like carbon dioxide, uric acid, and ammonia, from your body.

Getting Warmer

The best time to **stretch muscles** is when they are **warm.** If you stretch cold muscles, you can **tear** or **strain** them, so it's best to warm up first.

DID YOU KNOW?

A muscle can **STRETCH** up to **10 TIMES** its normal length.

A Good Stretch

One of the most popular exercises that involves stretching is yoga. Yoga has been shown to have many physical benefits and can help decrease injuries. It also has many mental benefits, such as stress relief and greater focus.

A Flexible Definition

Increased flexibility from stretching doesn't necessarily make your muscles longer or change their shape, but it will get your body used to moving through a greater range of motion. This helps your nervous system stop sending painful distress signals to your brain when you try to deepen a stretch.

Stretching Limits

Women tend to be **more flexible** than men, though the amount of flexibility varies from person to person. **Flexibility** tends to **decrease as we age,** mostly due to a decrease in our activity levels.

Now That's a Stretch!

Most experts agree you should **hold a stretch** for **15** to **30 seconds.** If you feel pain, stop! The best way to stretch is to breathe deeply while you hold the stretch; stop when you feel the muscle tense; then relax your muscles and repeat, trying to reach a little farther than you did the first time.

It takes a lot of time and effort to create a vaccine. Vaccine creation involves scientists, researchers, and experts from all over the world. Research sometimes takes 10 to 15 years before the vaccine can be made public.
The first stages alone may last several years.

PLAYING DEFENSE

An antigen is the part of a bacterium or virus that your immune system can identify and attack, preventing it from making you sick. Vaccines work by killing the antigen so it doesn't cause illness and by telling your immune system to make antibodies that will protect you from getting sick if you are exposed to disease.

Holy Cow!

In 1796, Edward Jenner used cowpox material to create a kind of smallpox vaccine. While his method was updated over the next 200 years, his first vaccine technologies were the starting point for the vaccination that is believed to have completely wiped out smallpox.

Rabid Growth

In 1885, Louis Pasteur created a rabies vaccine. This quickly led to progress in the development of effective vaccines, including vaccines against tetanus, diphtheria, plague, cholera, anthrax, typhoid, and tuberculosis.

Chinese Medicine

Researchers have found proof that the Chinese used a vaccine to protect against smallpox as early as 1000 CE. This method of preventing the disease was practiced in Africa and Turkey as well, before spreading to Europe and the Americas. Smallpox was a contagious virus that caused a fever, a rash, and eventually led to death in many infected people.

Making Progress

Vaccine research and development increased during the middle of the 20th century. The clinical trial for the polio vaccine, created in 1952 by Jonas Salk and his team, was the biggest public health experiment in American history. Researchers successfully developed vaccines for other diseases commonly found in children, such as measles, mumps, and rubella.

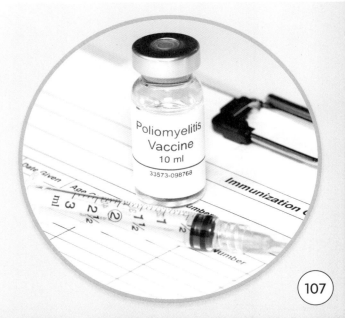

FUN FACTS about Vitamins

Vitamins were discovered between **1913** (vitamin A) and **1941** (folic acid).

Most vitamins **break down** when exposed to **light** and **heat**, so store your vitamins someplace **cool** and **dry**.

Oranges have plenty of vitamin C (around 50 mg), but **kiwis** and **strawberries** have almost **double** that amount.

2X

Collagen, which holds your cells together, is produced with help from vitamin C.

IF YOU GET A **CUT** OR **FRACTURE** A BONE, **VITAMIN C** HELPS YOU **HEAL.**

The **vitamin C** and **vitamin B** you ingest are **removed daily** through your urine, so you have to **replace** your vitamin C and vitamin B intake **every day**.

Your body produces energy with the help of B vitamins.

Vitamin E isn't just one vitamin; it's the name for a group of eight fat-soluble vitamins.

Most **vitamin D** supplements are made of **lanolin,** which is a fatty wax found naturally on **sheep's wool.**

You need 10,000 international units (IU) of vitamin D, which can be produced just by being outside in the sunlight. The lighter your skin, the faster you produce vitamin D. Where you live, time of day, and season all factor into how quickly your body makes vitamin D.

Food, Glorious Food

Things your body does every day— like playing, working, growing, and staying healthy—take fuel. This fuel comes from food, in the form of nutrients. Your body needs six different kinds of nutrients: proteins, carbohydrates, fats and oils, vitamins, minerals, and water.

Invite In Vitamins and Minerals

Vitamins and minerals help your body properly use other nutrients. They also help your body make new cells. Many different kinds of vitamins and minerals are needed for a wide range of functions.

BUILD YOURSELF UP!

Protein is important to your growth, because it works to build, keep up, and replace tissues in the body, as well as helping your body repair itself when it is hurt. Protein can be found throughout the body. In fact, our organs, muscles, and immune systems are mainly made up of protein.

protein protein

Fueling Up

CALORIES YOU BURN

CALORIES YOU EAT

Your body burns fuel, which it gets from food, to make energy. How much energy you get from food is measured by calories. When you exercise, you also burn calories.

Fat Chance

When you run out of carbohydrates to burn, your body turns to its fat stores for energy. In addition to providing more energy than carbohydrates, fat helps the body with other important functions, like protecting its organs and storing vitamins.

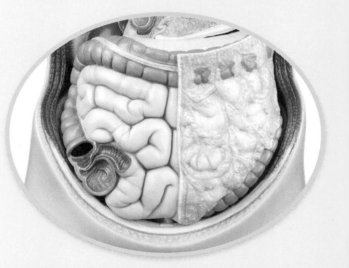

Sugar High

Your body gets energy primarily from carbohydrates. Carbohydrates are classified in different groups, such as sugars and starches. Sugar gives your body a quick jolt of energy, while the energy from starches lasts longer.

Drink Up!

Bodies of Water

Our bodies need water! We can only survive a few days without it. The things you do every day, like sweating, breathing, peeing, and pooping, wouldn't be possible without water. These same things also remove water from your body.

Out of Water

Dehydration occurs when there isn't enough water in your body. Dehydration can cause many problems in your body, including headaches, low energy, and exhaustion. If you become badly dehydrated, you may have to go to the hospital. To combat dehydration, make sure you're drinking plenty of water every day, especially if it's hot outside or if you are exercising.

Don't Forget to Hydrate!

On average, men need about 13 cups of water per day, and women need 9 cups. Don't wait until you feel thirsty to drink water, though. When your body senses you are thirsty, it means you've already lost about 1% of the water in your body.

Word Search
Nutrition

Look at the puzzle below and see if you can find these words all about nutrition. Circle the words going across, up and down, and diagonally. Some words may be backwards!

CALORIES	HYDRATE	SNACK
ENERGY	MEAL	STARCH
FAT	MINERAL	SUGAR
FOOD	PORTION	VITAMIN
FUEL	PROTEIN	WATER

```
L H E Q X O X H R C V F O O D
C B Y X A J G Y C I K D G G R
U G S D M M A A T R S E D N Z
Q K V R R D I A M D A N Z T N
J N P A L A M N F I C T S N O
E B R G Y I T X E C F H S R I
N H O U N W C E E R A U E L T
I V T S Y G R E N E A T E P R
S D E O B H W E S W A L L L O
G C I S C I X N T W A Z K D P
L P N J S N A M J Z R K L F M
V A D B L C M V B E E Z E A H
N X E B K P S V X G S B Q T W
D B Y M V Q T A R E D Z T Z S
C A L O R I E S K Y T E M V M
```

Answers on page 307

Kidneys

Most people have two of these bean-shaped organs in their bodies. You have one kidney on each side of your spine. The kidneys sit behind your stomach, and they help keep you healthy by balancing the composition of your blood.

Filter Feeders

The kidneys serve as a filtering system for your blood. Kidneys are made up of millions of smaller filters called nephrons. The nephrons remove extra water and toxins from the blood, and in doing so create between 1 and 2 quarts of urine each day.

A Balancing Act

When your blood is filtered by your kidneys, not all of the chemicals in it get sent to your bladder as urine. The kidneys are able to save healthy amounts of chemicals called electrolytes, like sodium, potassium, and phosphorus, that your body still needs. They send these back into your blood, which helps your body maintain the perfect balance of necessary chemicals.

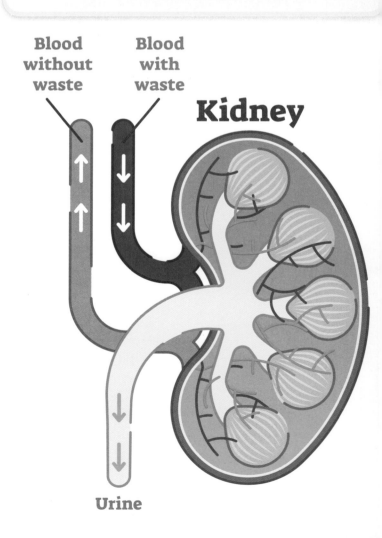

Blood without waste

Blood with waste

Kidney

Urine

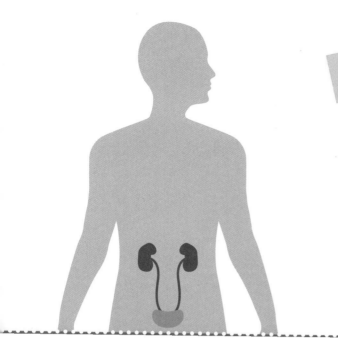

In addition to their job as filters, kidneys are also responsible for releasing three different hormones: erythropoietin, which tells your bone marrow to make red blood cells; renin, which regulates your blood pressure; and active vitamin D, which regulates your calcium levels.

Be Sure to Water Your Beans

One of the most important things to do to keep your kidneys healthy is to stay hydrated. Water helps kidneys rid the body of toxins. Keeping your blood pressure low, exercising regularly, and eating a low-fat diet also may help keep your kidneys running smoothly.

Don't Cell Yourself Short Inside Your Cells

Your body is made of billions of cells, which are the tiny units that make up all living things. Inside every one of these is a whole world full of many pieces that work together to keep the cell functioning smoothly.

The Brains Behind Your Brain

Cells are full of organelles, which are specialized parts of the cell that perform different functions, like organs in the human body. One of those is the nucleus, the central hub where DNA is located, which is protected by a nuclear membrane. The nucleus is like the brain of a cell, with the instructions for making all the other parts.

The Powerhouse of the Cell

Mitochondria are the pieces of the cell that turn our food into usable power, using oxygen to convert sugar into energy, which takes the form of adenosine triphosphate (ATP). This process is called cellular respiration.

A Smooth Start

Endoplasmic reticulum, which is made of folded membrane, comes in two types: smooth and rough. Smooth endoplasmic reticulum (shown in blue) is where fats, called lipids, are made. Rough endoplasmic reticulum (shown in yellow), studded with small, round molecules called ribosomes, is responsible for making proteins.

Get Where You're Golgi-ng

The Golgi apparatus, also called the Golgi body or the Golgi complex, works like a tiny post office in each of your cells. Its job is to sort and send proteins and lipids to different parts of the cell in packages called vesicles.

CONSCIENTIOUS CONSUMERS

Lysosomes are the garbage disposals of the cell. They process waste created by the cells, using specific enzymes to break down old cell parts, microorganisms, and macromolecules like proteins. Lysosomes recycle, too! Many parts of the material they digest can be reused by the cell.

The History of Antibiotics

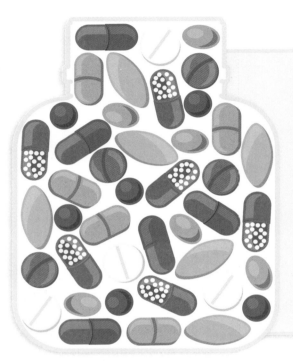

CENTURY'S FINEST

Considered one of the most important medical discoveries of the 20th century, the development of antibiotics has allowed doctors to treat illnesses that had been considered life-threatening in the past. The body has a strong immune system, but without antibiotics, some germs—like the bacteria that cause pneumonia—can be serious.

BREAKING THE MOLD

A British scientist named Alexander Fleming is credited with discovering penicillin, which is widely considered the first antibiotic. This breakthrough happened by accident! Fleming was doing laboratory work at St. Mary's Hospital in London when he found a natural substance that was able to attack a type of bacterium called *Staphylococcus aureus*. He noticed that colonies of this particular bacterium had been destroyed when a certain Penicillium mold grew near it. He concluded that something about the Penicillium mold could kill *Staphylococcus* bacteria. He named that substance "penicillin" after the mold that made it. He won the Nobel Prize in 1945 for discovering penicillin.

Trending

After Alexander Fleming's discovery, scientists around the world started making penicillin. Tests showed that small amounts of penicillin were strong enough to kill serious infections, saving the lives of many people.

OUT TO BATTLE

Penicillin was used on the battlefields of World War II to treat wounds, prevent infections, and cure diseases like pneumonia. By the late 1940s, the general public started using penicillin to treat illness and infection.

Picking Up Prescriptions

The introduction of penicillin paved the way for the production of dozens more antibiotics. Today, antibiotics are prescribed and purchased with great regularity. Nearly 150 million prescriptions for antibiotics are written yearly by doctors in the United States.

How Antibiotics Work

If you have a bacterial infection, you need antibiotics. An antibiotic is a medicine that kills bacteria, which are small organisms (made of a single cell!) that can grow and live anywhere.

Teamwork

Antibiotics work with your body to rid it of a bacterial infection. When you are sick, your body makes antibodies to fight off the infection. Antibiotics help by finding the bacteria and either stopping their growth or destroying them. Then your immune system gets rid of the dead bacteria.

Not Going Viral

Antibiotics don't kill viruses, like the common cold or the stomach flu. Because your immune system can typically fight viruses on its own, doctors don't usually prescribe antibiotics if you are sick from a virus.

Putting Up a Fight

Antibiotic resistance is a threat to the effectiveness of antibiotics. Over time, antibiotics have been used so much that some kinds no longer work the way they are supposed to against the bacteria they were designed to destroy. Sometimes bacteria outsmart the antibiotic, so a different kind of antibiotic has to be used, or a larger dose must be given in order for the antibiotic to work.

STAY THE COURSE

You need to take the entire course of antibiotics prescribed by your doctor. Sometimes, you can start to feel better before you are done with the antibiotics, but if you stop taking them, the bacteria can continue to grow inside your body, making you even sicker.

Side Effects May Include...

While antibiotics do many good things for your body, they may also attack good bacteria, which can cause **nausea** and other problems. **Allergic reactions** can also occur. Some people experience **rashes** when they take certain antibiotics.

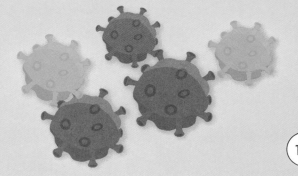

(Not so) FUN FACTS about the Flu

"FLU" is the name we commonly use to talk about **influenza**, a virus that infects your **respiratory system**.

ONCE YOU HAVE A **PARTICULAR STRAIN**, OR TYPE, OF FLU, YOU MOST LIKELY **WON'T GET IT AGAIN.** YOUR BODY HAS ALREADY MADE **ANTIBODIES** TO **PROTECT YOU** FROM THAT TYPE OF FLU.

If many people get the flu in a certain geographic region, it's called an epidemic. If a large number of people worldwide get the flu, it's called a pandemic.

The **flu virus** **mutates**, or **changes**, every year, so even with **protective antibodies**, you may get another version of the flu **again**.

Flu season is usually **October** to **May**, which means people are more likely to become **sick** with the flu during those months.

THE FLU IS CONTAGIOUS A DAY BEFORE SYMPTOMS SHOW, AND FOR ABOUT FIVE TO SEVEN DAYS AFTER.

The flu is contagious—
it spreads when a sick person sneezes, coughs, or talks, or if a healthy person touches an object that has flu virus on it and then touches his or her mouth, nose, or eyes.

FLU SYMPTOMS INCLUDE:

high fever

sore throat

cough

headaches

muscle aches

Usually, healthy people don't have any **complications** from the flu and will begin to **feel better within a week** of becoming sick.

In addition to washing your hands to prevent the spread of the flu, doctors recommend you get the flu vaccine every year. The vaccine helps your body create antibodies that can attack the flu virus if you come into contact with it.

Medical Myths

Myth: Ulcers from Spice, Stress, and Life

Ulcers are not caused by spicy foods, stress, or lifestyle choices. Most ulcers are caused by a type of bacterium called *Helicobacter pylori*. They can also be caused by certain medications or supplements, like iron tablets and aspirin.

Myth: Seven-Year Stay

If you swallow chewing gum, it doesn't stay in your system for long. Many people believe it stays there for seven years, but this isn't true. Some of the ingredients in gum are indigestible, but so is plant fiber. Your digestive system works on gum the same way it works on the food you eat; whatever can't be absorbed is moved through the digestive system and then out of your body.

Myth: Losing Sight in the Dark

Sitting too close to the television or reading in the dark may make your eyes hurt or feel uncomfortable because they are working harder than usual, but neither habit ruins your eyesight or causes you to need glasses. However, if you often stare at the TV or computer in such close range that your eyes hurt, you may be nearsighted and need glasses.

Myth: Tiring Turkey

Eating turkey doesn't make you any sleepier than eating chicken or beef. Turkey contains a chemical called tryptophan, which can cause tiredness, but a smaller portion of other meats contains just as much tryptophan as the Thanksgiving bird. You may feel more tired after a big holiday meal because you've eaten too much...of everything!

MYTH: HOT HEAD

While it's a good idea to bundle up in cold weather, wearing a hat doesn't completely prevent your overall body heat loss. Many people think that most of your body heat escapes through your head, but you only lose about 7% to 10% of your total body heat from that area. The amount you lose through your head is proportional to the amount of skin on your head compared to the amount of skin on your body.

MYTH: COLDS FROM THE COLD

Cold weather won't make you sick. When you are cold, you may feel sicker because you are chilled, but you're no more likely to get sick in a cold environment than in a warm one. However, studies have shown that the viruses that cause the common cold and flu may spread more easily in colder temperatures.

Color Blindness

OFF-COLOR

People with color vision deficiency see colors differently than most people. Severe forms of color vision deficiency are known as color blindness. Sometimes, people who are color-blind don't even know it unless they are tested—they aren't aware that there are differences among colors.

NOT SO BLACK AND WHITE

There are **three different** kinds of **color blindness,** which range from common to rare. Color blindness is caused by differences in the parts of the eye that respond to the colors **blue, green,** and **red.** The types of color blindness are **red-green,** which is most common, **blue-yellow,** and **total color blindness,** which is rare.

Keep an Eye on This

It's estimated that 8% of men and 0.5% of women have the most common form of color blindness. While it is usually an inherited condition, damage to parts of the eye and aging can cause color blindness. Inherited color bli can happen at birth, or it can start in childhood cases, people develop color blindness as a

More men are color-blind than women. This is because the most common form of color blindness—red-green—is inherited through your genes, and the genes that carry color blindness are on the X chromosome. Women have two X chromosomes, so one chromosome without the gene for color blindness can cancel out the other. Men only have one X chromosome, so the gene can't be canceled out in the same way. The color blindness gene is passed down in an "X-linked" pattern, which mostly affects men.

Passing with Flying Colors

People with most forms of color blindness can live a normal life, even though there is no cure. Certain types of lenses can be used for people with red-green color blindness to help them correctly see colors. Recently, iPhone and iPad apps have been developed to help people with color blindness determine which colors are which.

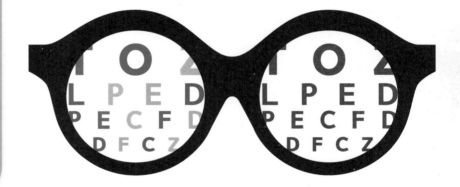

Full Spectrum

Red-green color blindness, such as deuteranopia and protanopia, causes red to look dark green, and orange and green to look yellowish. In blue-yellow color blindness such as tritanopia, green looks blue, and red, orange, and yellow look pink.

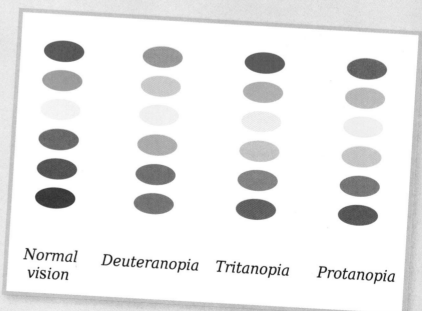

Normal vision   Deuteranopia   Tritanopia   Protanopia

Body by Numbers

Scientists measure the body in many different ways.
Here are some of their fascinating findings!

Humans shed about 77 pounds of skin particles over the course of a lifetime!

The average head weighs 10 pounds.

YOUR BLOOD **TRAVELS** 12,000 MILES THROUGH YOUR **VESSELS** IN ONE DAY. THAT WOULD BE LIKE TRAVELING FROM **NEW YORK** TO **CALIFORNIA** FOUR TIMES.

Blood makes a full circuit of the body in about one minute.

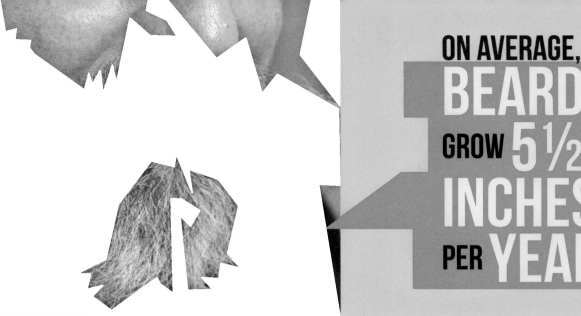

ON AVERAGE, **BEARDS** GROW **5 ½ INCHES** PER **YEAR.**

Throughout your life, you will produce enough saliva to fill 53 bathtubs to the brim.

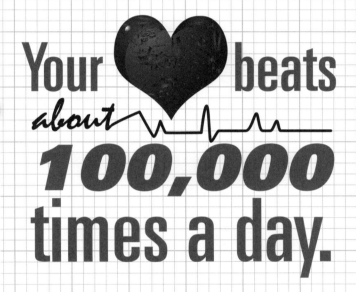

Your ❤ beats about **100,000** times a day.

If all the **blood vessels** in a child's body were laid out end to end, they would total about **60,000 miles—** long enough to circle the world more than **twice!**

Oh, My Aching Head!

There are more than 150 different types of headaches! Some common forms of headaches are: tension headaches, sinus headaches, migraines, cluster headaches, and hormonal headaches. Headaches are caused when blood vessel and head muscle nerves send pain indicators to your brain, but nobody really knows why this happens.

Tension　　**Migraine**　　**Sinus**　　**Cluster**　　**Hormonal**

STRESS GIVING ME A HEADACHE

Many different factors can cause a headache. Some of the most common triggers are stress; not eating or sleeping enough; straining your eyes, neck, or back; certain allergens, like strong perfumes or cigarette smoke; intense noise or lighting; and changes in the weather.

My Head Hurts!

By the age of seven, more than 40% of children have complained of a headache. About 4% of children complain of frequently having headaches. By age 15, almost 75% of children and teens have reported experiencing a headache.

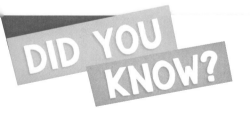

Ancient Medicine

In ancient Greece and Rome, people used a variety of natural plants and herbs to treat their headaches. They drank peppermint tea and mixtures of rosemary, lavender, and chamomile. They even put raw potato, onion, and cabbage on their heads to try to get rid of the pain!

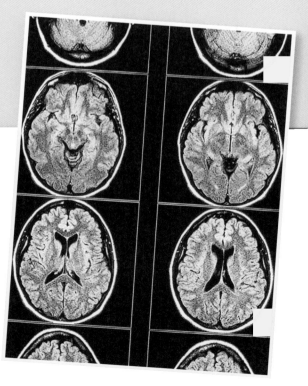

Common Headaches

THAT'S INTENSE

One of the most common types of headaches is the tension headache. Unlike a migraine, where pain is located mostly on one side of the head, tension headaches wrap around your head, causing pain on both sides. They can happen every once in a while, or even every day.

CLUSTER TOGETHER

Cluster headaches get their name from their tendency to happen daily over the span of a cluster of a few weeks or months. They cause extreme pain on the side of the head, which can also impact the eyes, nose, or other parts of the face, and they last from a few minutes to a few hours. Cluster headaches are more common in men than in women and are generally less common overall than other types of headaches.

OUCH!

When your sinuses become inflamed, you can develop a third, common type of headache—a sinus headache. Sinus headaches can be caused by bacteria or a virus, like the common cold. If you experience a sinus headache, you likely will feel pain around your cheeks, forehead, nose, and eyes, where your sinuses are located. You might also have a fever or other cold-like symptoms.

Crossword Puzzle
Headaches

Complete the crossword using the clues below.
For help, look at the pages of headache facts!

ACROSS

3. Ancient Greeks and Romans drank mixes of lavender, chamomile, and _____ to treat headaches

8. Pain that results from looking at light

9. The most complex organ in the human body

DOWN

1. A painful sensation occurring in the head

2. A painful headache located mostly on the side of the head

4. The ability to see

5. One of the most common types of headaches

6. Headaches that happen daily for days or weeks at a time

7. This type of headache can be caused by a virus or bacteria

Answers on page 308

FUN FACTS about Doctors

When you say you are going to the doctor, what do you really mean? There are hundreds of specialty areas of medicine; most doctors focus their studies and then their practices on a specialty. Here are some common types of doctors.

Allergists and immunologists treat asthma, food and seasonal allergies, and autoimmune diseases—diseases that happen when your immune system accidentally attacks healthy cells in the body.

Anesthesiologists administer the medicine to numb you to keep you from feeling pain, or put you under during medical procedures like surgery.

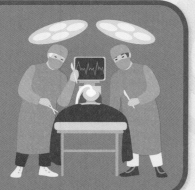

Dermatologists are doctors who treat problems related to the skin, from acne to skin cancer.

Hematologists are specialists in treating blood diseases and conditions dealing with the lymphatic system.

Family physicians are doctors who see children and adults for routine tests and regular checkups.

Neurologists are doctors trained to treat conditions that start in the nervous system, like Parkinson's disease and Alzheimer's disease.

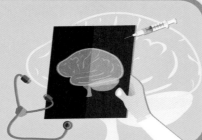

Obstetricians and gynecologists, sometimes known as OB/GYNs, deal primarily with women's health, reproductive issues, and pregnancy and childbirth.

 **Ophthalmologists are doctors who diagnose and treat all aspects of the eye, including performing eye surgery.**

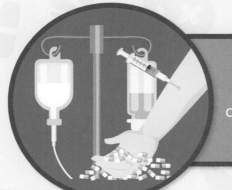 Oncologists help diagnose and treat patients with cancer.

Pediatricians are doctors who primarily see young patients, from birth through the teenage years.

Podiatrists take care of your feet and any associated injuries, conditions, or diseases.

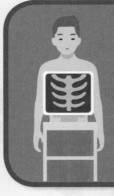

Psychiatrists see patients with disorders that change or affect their behavior, such as depression and anxiety.

Radiologists use imaging tests, like X-rays and ultrasounds, to diagnose and treat diseases.

Alternative Medicine

Some people believe the body can be cured without synthetic medications, so they practice a type of medicine called homeopathy. Homeopathic doctors use small amounts of plants, minerals, or other natural substances to help the whole body heal instead of focusing on a single part.

Like Cures Like

Homeopathy started in Germany at the end of the 18th century, founded by a German doctor named Samuel Hahnemann. Hahnemann believed that if you were sick with a stomachache, for example, and were given a medicine that would cause an otherwise healthy person to get a stomachache, that medicine could cure you because it wakes up the body's natural defense system. This led to a concept he called "like cures like," which has become a commonly used phrase when describing homeopathic medicine.

Working Hard or Hardly Working?

Homeopathic remedies are used to treat a variety of ailments, from allergies to arthritis, but doctors can't agree on whether they work. Some studies have shown that these remedies do work, but some doctors note that these results might be because of the placebo effect. The placebo effect is what happens when a person starts to feel better solely because he or she believes the treatment is working, even if the treatment itself has no effect.

PINS AND NEEDLES

Acupuncture—a method of traditional Chinese medicine—is a complementary and alternative medical procedure that involves inserting needles into the skin, usually to ease pain or relieve stress. Some people believe that these thin acupuncture needles, placed in certain areas of the body, balance the body's energy, while others believe the needles trigger your body's natural pain relievers by stimulating nerves and muscles.

Compliments to Complementary Medicine

Complementary and alternative medicine—medicine outside of conventional, or common, medical practice, including homeopathy—is as popular today as ever. A study found that more than 30% of all adults and more than 10% of children had used some sort of complementary or alternative medicine in the last year, including dietary supplements, acupuncture (shown below), and massage.

137

Systems of the Body
Immune System

TO THE RESCUE

Your immune system is your body's superhero! Because unwelcome guests like viruses and bacteria can easily enter the body and live there, causing you to get sick, the tissues, cells, and organs of the immune system have to work hard to fight infection and keep you healthy.

STRESSING ME OUT

Certain things can compromise your immune system, making you more prone to illness. One of those things is stress. When you experience stress, your body produces more cortisol, which is a hormone your body needs for everyday life. However, if you produce too much cortisol, it can weaken your immune system, making you more likely to get sick. Not sleeping enough can also impact your immune system.

Getting a BOOST

Your immune system works with vaccines to help you stay healthy. When you get a vaccine for chicken pox, for example, the vaccine encourages your immune system to make antibodies to fight the chicken pox virus. That way, if you are exposed to the chicken pox virus later, your body will recognize it and be able to fight against it.

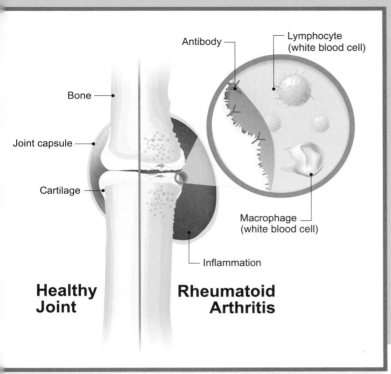

Antibody

Lymphocyte
(white blood cell)

Bone

Joint capsule

Cartilage

Macrophage
(white blood cell)

Inflammation

**Healthy
Joint**

**Rheumatoid
Arthritis**

On the Attack

Sometimes, the immune system can attack itself, causing an autoimmune disease. This happens when the body's white blood cells can't tell the difference between normal cells and abnormal cells, so they start attacking the healthy cells. While nearly 8% of the United States population has an autoimmune disease, women tend to be affected more than men. Autoimmune diseases include rheumatoid arthritis, Crohn's disease, and more than 80 other conditions.

Older and Wiser

You may get more colds than your parents. The older a person gets, the more they have come into contact with germs. An older person's body understands that when it senses a virus or bacterium, it needs to immediately create the antibodies necessary to fight it.

A Little Dirt Can't Hurt

There might be such a thing as being too clean. If you clean too much and destroy all viruses and bacteria, your immune system may not properly develop. If your body has never been exposed to viruses or bacteria, it will have a hard time developing the antibodies it needs to fight the virus or bacteria if you come into contact with them again. Experts say it's important to wash hands and practice proper hygiene but not so much that you actually destroy the good bacteria, too.

DID YOU KNOW?

It's possible that **positive emotions** and an **optimistic attitude** can help **boost your immune system.** This may happen because **positive** people are more likely to **treat their bodies well, eat healthy foods,** and be **less stressed.**

Health Care Professionals

A Figure of Speech

Some people have trouble making certain sounds and may seek out the help of a speech-language pathologist (SLP), also known as a speech therapist. A speech therapist is trained in the development of communication and speech and language disorder. A trained, licensed speech therapist evaluates a person's speech, language, communication and mouth (chewing, swallowing) functions. He or she identifies and treats problems with a person's ability to communicate.

Body of Work

Like a medical doctor (MD), a doctor of osteopathy (DO) is licensed and can practice all types of medicine. DOs focus on a person's entire body, as well as their environment and lifestyle, to help prevent illness and treat symptoms.

THERE'S THE RUB

Whether on the advice of a medical professional or simply to reduce stress and tension in their muscles, many people seek out the help of a massage therapist. A massage therapist uses her or his hands to knead, press, and manipulate the body's soft tissues, which include muscles, tendons, ligaments, and connective tissues. There are many different types of massage, from deep tissue to Swedish. They all fall under two categories: rehabilitative massage, also known as medical or clinical massage, which is performed in a hospital or clinic; and relaxation massage, which is performed at a wellness center or spa.

A Necessary Occupation

If people have trouble doing everyday things, like working or feeding themselves, they might work with an occupational therapist. Occupational therapists work with people of all ages to help them perform daily tasks in a way that works with their limitations—so an occupational therapist might adapt an activity to fit a patient's particular challenge.

The Best Medicine

Pharmacists are experts in medicines. They work with a person's doctor to determine and provide the best course of medication for his or her condition. They educate people about their medications, and explain whether or not the medications could interfere with anything else they are taking, like other medications or supplements. Pharmacists commonly work in drugstores, but they also can be found in hospitals, clinics, and nursing homes.

MOVING FORWARD

If someone is injured, she or he might seek the help of a physical therapist (PT). These health care professionals work with their patients to help them move better and help minimize any pain or discomfort associated with their injuries. PTs work not just in hospitals and clinics; they also work in homes, schools, sports facilities, and nursing homes.

Pediatric Medicine

Getting Schooled

Many years of schooling are required for pediatricians. To become a pediatrician, you will need to go through four years of an undergraduate program, four years of medical school, at least a year of a pediatric internship, and at least two years of a hospital residency for your chosen specialty.

It's in the Books

Even before Nils Rosen von Rosenstein wrote his book on pediatric medicine, there were four other books on the topic, the first of which was written in 1472. The first hospital devoted to caring for children was opened in Paris, France, in 1802. Other hospitals followed by adding pediatric wings to existing hospitals.

GROWING UP

One thing you will always find in a pediatric doctor's office is the pediatric growth chart. There are two widely accepted versions: one for children from birth to age two, and one for age two and older. Both of these growth charts have a series of arcs, or curves, that are meant to show how a child is growing in both height and weight. Pediatric growth charts were first developed in 1977.

Generally Speaking

While some pediatricians choose a specialty, like cardiology or surgery, many pediatricians serve as general doctors for their young patients. They examine their patients, order or perform any necessary testing, read test results, diagnose sickness, and prescribe medication and treatments. They also administer routine vaccinations and deal with emergencies like broken bones.

Systems of the Body

The lymphatic system is the garbage truck of your body. The network of tissues and organs that makes up this system helps the body get rid of waste, toxins, and other unwanted materials. It also moves lymph around the body. Lymph is a fluid that contains white blood cells, which help your body fight infection.

TRAVEL NETWORK

Lymph travels around the body through a network of lymph vessels much like blood travels around the body through blood vessels. Whereas blood carries nutrients and other substances into tissues, lymph vessels drain fluid from the tissues and transport it to the lymph nodes. These small, glandlike masses of tissue filter out and destroy bacteria and other harmful substances. The bigger lymph vessels then carry the cleaned fluid back to the superior vena cava vein, where it enters the bloodstream.

Lymph nodes

Small but Mighty

Lymph nodes are very small—usually about 1 centimeter across—and kidney-shaped or round. They are found in groups in the groin, armpit, and neck. Lymphocytes are a type of white blood cell. The two main types of lymphocytes, T cells and B cells, help your body fight infection. Although lymphocytes come from the bone marrow, they migrate to the lymph nodes, as well as the spleen and thymus.

SPLEEN by the NUMBERS

Generally, the **spleen** is located in the **left upper part of your abdomen,** above your stomach and under your ribs. One of the ways you can remember this is to memorize the **1x3x5x7x9x11** rule: The spleen of an adult is **1 inch** by **3 inches** by **5 inches**; it **weighs** about **7 ounces**; and you can find it between your **ninth** and **eleventh ribs**!

Spleen

THAT'S SWOLLEN

Once the lymph nodes clean the lymph fluid and remove things like bacteria, the lymph fluid is transported back into the bloodstream via the veins. When you are sick, infection gathers in the lymph nodes, causing them to swell. For example, if you go to the doctor with a sore throat, the doctor will check for swollen glands, which are the swollen lymph nodes in your neck.

Cleanup Crew

As you breathe, substances like extra water and proteins leak out of your capillaries— your smallest blood vessels. If the lymphatic system didn't get rid of that fluid, your body would swell like a water balloon! Germs are cleaned out by the lymphocytes in the lymph nodes.

DID YOU KNOW?

The spleen is part of the lymphatic system, but you don't need it to live. The spleen is soft and made up of two kinds of tissue: Red pulp tissue separates out red blood cells that are unusable because they are damaged or old, and white pulp tissue uses T cells and B cells to fight infection.

Stick It Out

Your tongue has many different uses. It helps make changes in sound when you speak and cleans teeth after eating. Your tongue can even help prevent you from getting sick. Your tonsils, groups of tissue in the back part of your tongue as well as on either side, work to filter out germs that can cause infection in your body.

Tonsils

Tongue

Speaking in Different Tongues

Women generally have slightly shorter tongues than men, but the average length of the human tongue is about 3 inches. Tongues are measured from back to front, or from the epiglottis— a flap of cartilage in the back of the mouth—to the tip.

Purple Tongue

Did you ever notice that the bottom of your tongue is purple?

You have a lot of **blood vessels** running along the bottom of your tongue, and they are what gives it a **purple color**.

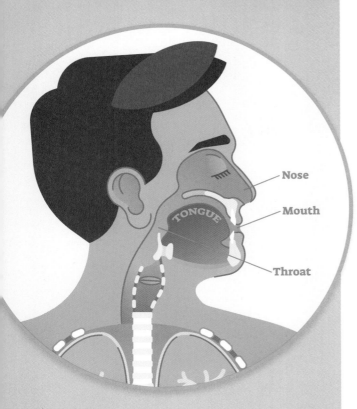

Nose

Mouth

Throat

Tongue Twister

Tongue muscles are either intrinsic or extrinsic. Intrinsic muscles aren't attached to a bone, and they help the tongue change shape. The extrinsic muscles are attached to the bone, allowing the tongue to move.

ONE TOUGH TONGUE

Your tongue is almost all muscle. In fact, your tongue is made up of eight muscles that work together so you can talk, eat, and swallow. These muscles are the only muscles in the entire human body that work independently of the skeleton.

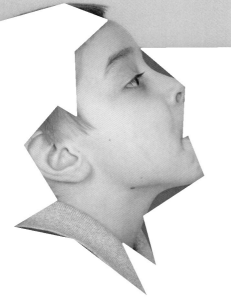

Blood Type

While everyone's blood has the same basic makeup of red and white cells, platelets, and plasma, different blood has different surface markers, which are found on the red cells and tell your body that the blood in your body belongs in your system. These surface markers are made of proteins and sugars, and are also called cell surface antigens. Your blood type is determined by your surface markers.

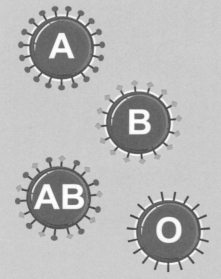

MARK MY WORDS

Certain blood types respond differently to transfusions. If you have AB blood, it means you have both A and B markers. People with AB blood can get A, B, AB, or O blood. If you have O blood, you can only receive O blood. Having O blood means you don't have A or B markers, so your body will fight A, B, and AB blood.

Know Your Type

It's important for people to know their blood types, especially if they are receiving transfusions. A transfusion is the process doctors use to give blood or components of blood to patients who have lost some of their own blood. When new blood enters someone's system, the body tries to recognize it—if it's the wrong blood type, the antibodies that the body produces to protect against unknown cells will attack the new blood.

The Rh Factor

Some people have Rh factor in their blood, which is another type of marker. Blood groups—A, B, AB, and O—and Rh factor combine to form eight main blood types. Your Rh factor is either positive or negative, meaning you have Rh factor or you don't. These markers are simply genetic differences—they don't determine anything about the quality of your blood.

O Marks the Spot

There is one type of blood that is considered universal. Type O negative blood can be given to anyone, regardless of blood type, because it has none of the markers that will cause the body receiving the blood to reject it. Type O negative blood is always in high demand in blood banks because it can be used for anyone in need. People with AB positive blood are universal recipients, meaning their blood has all the markers so they can receive any type.

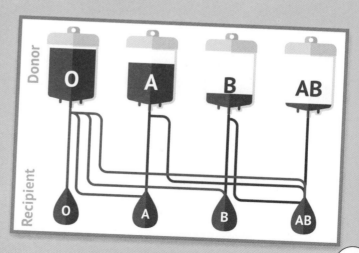

Search & Find®

The Gym

As part of a healthy lifestyle, it's important to keep your body moving! While some people like to fit in regular physical activity at home or outdoors, others prefer to get exercise at their local gyms, where they can use equipment like weights, treadmills, and exercise bikes to help boost their workouts.

Search & Find® these items you might find when exercising at the gym:

Boxing gloves

Dumbbell

Exercise ball

Exercise bike

Hand grip

Jump rope

Treadmill

Water bottle

WATER

WATER

Vital Signs

GIVE ME A SIGN

The body performs a series of basic functions, known as vital signs. When you go to the doctor's office, the doctor will check four main vital signs: body temperature, pulse rate, respiration—or breathing—rate, and blood pressure. These signs are helpful indicators when determining if a person is healthy or if there is a medical problem.

To a Certain Degree

The average healthy human body temperature is 98.6°F, but normal temperature ranges from 97.8°F to 99°F. It varies from person to person, and it can even vary depending on time of day, what you eat, whether you are male or female, and the activities you do. Your temperature is measured with a thermometer, which can read your temperature at different places on your body, like in your mouth and in your ear.

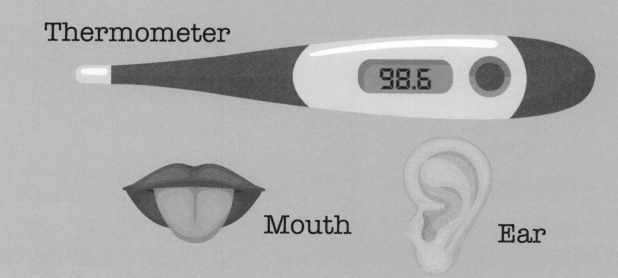

Thermometer

98.6

Mouth

Ear

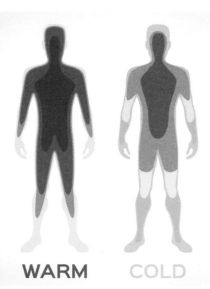

WARM   COLD

Feeling the Beat

The number of times your heart beats per minute is called your pulse rate. You can also measure your heart rhythm and the strength of your pulse. Your pulse can be faster or slower depending on your gender, your activity level, if you are sick, and your emotions.

By Degrees

What does it mean when your body temperature is abnormal? If it's too high, you have a fever. If it's too low, you may be experiencing hypothermia. Although a fever happens whenever your body is above its normal temperature, a person is not considered to have a significant fever until the temperature is above 100.4°F. Hypothermia happens when your body temperature drops below 95°F.

TAKE A BREATH

When you breathe, you take a certain number of breaths per minute—this is your respiration rate. Respiration rate is usually taken when a person is resting. You count the number of breaths you take in one minute, which is typically 12 to 16 breaths. Your respiration rate can change depending on how you feel or because of medical issues such as asthma.

Everyday Medical Aids

HEAR, HEAR

In the 1950s, the first electronic hearing aid was created. In the 60 years since, these devices have become smaller and more complicated, and in 2018 cost anywhere from $1,500 to $5,000. Even with advancements in the technology used in hearing aids, scientists continue looking for ways to help people hear, especially in crowded rooms or places where there is background noise.

I HEAR YOU

A hearing aid is placed behind or inside of the ear to magnify sounds for people who experience hearing loss. Unlike glasses, which can help you see with perfect vision, hearing aids can't give you perfect hearing. While hearing aids can't reverse hearing loss, they do help your ability to hear, listen, and communicate.

The reading stone—a piece of glass used to magnify things—is widely considered the first vision aid before glasses. It was invented in 1000 AD. The first pair of sunglasses was made of quartz and developed in China in the 12th century. While contact lenses are considered a modern invention, the first set of vision correcting lenses, developed in 13th century Italy, were more like contact lenses than glasses—they were placed directly in the eyes instead of in front of them!

VISUAL AID

The Wheel Deal

The first wheelchairs were actually wheelbarrows, used in ancient China to transport people and things. Two mechanical engineers—one disabled, one not—developed the first modern wheelchair. It was collapsible and made of steel. Their design is still used today, though it has been updated and improved. Wheelchairs can be used for everyday activities, and there are special wheelchairs for playing sports such as basketball, soccer, and diving.

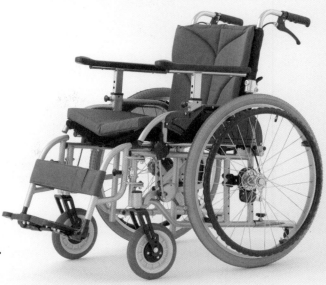

A Vision in White and Red

People who are blind and have other visual impairments, or vision problems, often walk with a white cane. This cane was developed in 1930 when the president of the Lions Club in Peoria, Illinois, saw a blind man carrying a black cane while crossing the street. People driving couldn't see the cane, so canes were painted white with a red stripe to make them more visible.

Walk This Way ⟶

Unlike the white cane used by visually impaired people, a walking cane is used for balance and stability. Not to be confused with a walking stick, which is used for activities like hiking, a walking cane is usually used by injured or elderly people. There are different kinds of canes: single-point (one leg and foot), tripod (one leg and three feet), and quad (one leg and four feet). Tripods and quads provide more stability.

155

Modern vs. Historical Treatments

Ancient people had no modern tools to diagnose illnesses, so how could they tell what was making someone sick? In the ancient civilization of Mesopotamia, medical healers would sacrifice sheep and examine the livers. It was thought that human blood came from the liver, so analyzing the liver—even a sheep's liver—was thought to give clues about human illness.

A Tonic Addiction

Tonics were, in some cases, a precursor to medicines. In Italy in 1863, a chemist came up with a tonic that contained red wine and coca leaves. It became very popular, in part because coca leaves contain cocaine, an addictive drug. This tonic, called Vin Mariani, was popular not just in Italy but around the world, inspiring the creation of a similarly popular product in the United States—Coca-Cola.

Speechless

Hemiglossectomy—which means full or partial amputation of the tongue—is a surgery performed today to successfully treat tongue cancer. If you lived in the 18th and 19th centuries, though, the surgery was performed to treat stuttering! It didn't work, and some patients bled to death.

PICK YOUR POISON

Some patients throughout history have picked their poison—literally—as a treatment for all kinds of ailments. Arsenic, which is known to be poisonous, was used as a cure in Chinese medicine, and as a treatment for diseases like malaria and arthritis all the way up to the 1950s. Cosmetics used by women in Victorian times also contained arsenic.

IN THE SAME MOLD

Since ancient Egyptian times, people have been using mold—specifically moldy bread—to disinfect wounds and cuts. While this may seem odd, it's not that crazy: It's a widely known fact that certain molds and fungi can stop the bacteria that cause disease.

PLAGUED BY THE SMELL

"Black Death" was another name for the plague that struck Europe in the 1300s and killed roughly half the population. At that time, doctors thought the plague was caused by deadly vapors, or gases, in the air. They also believed that you could fight vapors with vapors, so they encouraged people to store their farts in jars and sniff the therapeutic stink to avoid getting the plague!

Anatomical Terms

MANUS
Relating to the hand

BRACHIA
Relating to the arm

FEMORAL
Relating to the thigh

PEDAL
Relating to the foot

OCCIPITAL
Relating to the back of the head

CERVICAL
Relating to the neck

DORSAL
Relating to the back

VERTEBRAL
Relating to the vertebrae,
or segments of the spine

DIGITAL
Relating to the fingers

GLUTEAL
Relating to the gluteus, or buttocks

SURAL
Relating to the calf

CALCANEAL
Relating to the ankle

Conjoined Twins

Twinning

Conjoined twins are twins of the same gender who are joined together somewhere on their bodies, and they are typically female. These twins are sometimes known as Siamese twins, named for a pair of conjoined twins born in 1811 in Thailand, which used to be called Siam. Their names were Eng and Chang Bunker, and they lived to be 63 years old.

Twin Types

There are different forms of conjoined twins, depending on where they are joined. The most common are: *thoracopagus*, joined at the chest; *omphalopagus*, joined near the belly button; *pygopagus*, joined back to back; *ischiopagus*, joined at the pelvis; and *craniopagus*, joined at the head.

GOING SEPARATE WAYS

Even if they are joined at the head, conjoined twins can be separated. The first successful operation to separate craniopagus twins happened in 1955 in Chicago. How successful the surgery is depends on where the twins are joined and which organs they share.

Crossword Puzzle

Twins

Complete the crossword using the clues below.
For help, look at the pages of twin facts!

ACROSS

1. The organ that provides a growing fetus with nourishment from its mother

6. Twins who share the same genetics

7. The female reproductive cell

8. A female sibling

9. Many twins are born early, or _____

10. A fluid-filled pouch where a fetus grows

DOWN

2. Two children born from the same mother at the same time

3. Twins who are joined together

4. Twins who develop from two separate fertilized eggs

5. A male sibling

The Lady with the Lamp
Florence Nightingale

Lighting the Way

Florence Nightingale was a nurse in the 1800s. She is well-known for being a leader in health care and for changing policies around proper standards of medical care at that time, which influenced future practices. She is sometimes called "The Lady with the Lamp" because she carried a lamp when she made nighttime rounds to help the wounded.

Early Aspirations

Florence Nightingale was named for Florence, Italy, the city in which she was born in 1820. She was born to wealthy British parents who disliked the fact that their daughter knew, from a young age, that she wanted to help people by becoming a nurse. She later defied her parents by enrolling in nursing school in Germany.

Hero's Journey

Once she finished nursing school, Nightingale was sent to Crimea in Eastern Europe during the Crimean War. When she and her fellow nurses arrived at the hospital in Crimea, they found unsanitary conditions that were killing the wounded soldiers faster than their injuries were. Nightingale scrubbed the hospital and started a laundry facility and a kitchen. Her efforts helped reduce the death rate of soldiers in the hospital by two-thirds.

All Hail Nightingale

Because of her efforts in Crimea, Nightingale came home to England as a hero. She was given a cash award and an engraved brooch from Queen Victoria, which was known as the "Nightingale Jewel." She used the money to establish St. Thomas' Hospital and the Nightingale Training School for Nurses.

Crimea

She Persisted

While in Crimea, Nightingale developed a bacterial infection from which she never recovered. Even though she lived to be 90 years old, she was bedridden and homebound for much of her later life. Still, she continued to work from her bed, and she died at her home after a brief illness in 1910.

She Could Manage

During the Civil War in the United States, Nightingale was often asked about how to manage the hospitals on the battlefields. She authored reports and books on the topic of running hospitals, and she was considered an expert on public sanitation, both in her home country of England and in India—even though she had never been to India.

Medical Milestones of the 19th Century

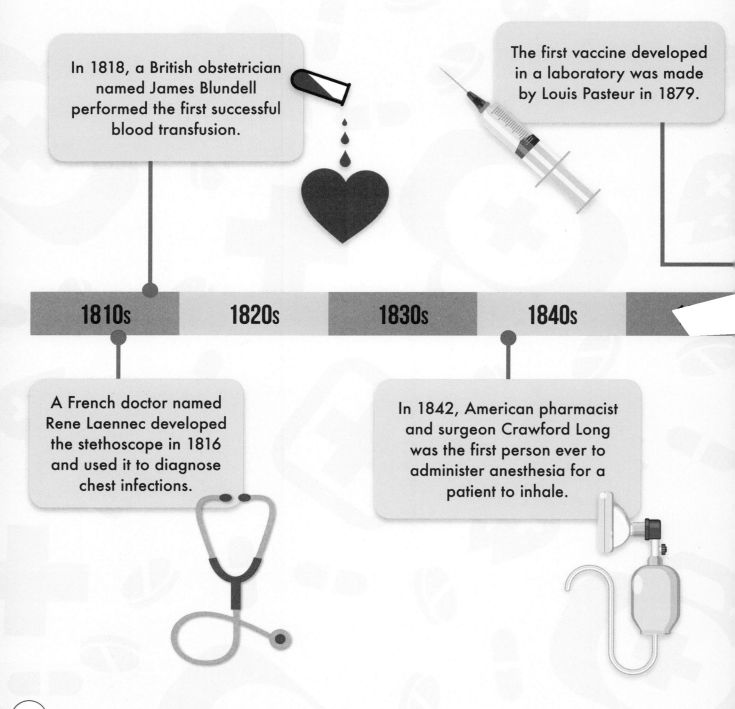

In 1818, a British obstetrician named James Blundell performed the first successful blood transfusion.

The first vaccine developed in a laboratory was made by Louis Pasteur in 1879.

1810s   **1820s**   **1830s**   **1840s**

A French doctor named Rene Laennec developed the stethoscope in 1816 and used it to diagnose chest infections.

In 1842, American pharmacist and surgeon Crawford Long was the first person ever to administer anesthesia for a patient to inhale.

In 1897, chemists working in a German company called Bayer AG invented aspirin.

The first rabies vaccine was given to a nine-year-old boy named Joseph Meister after he was bitten by a rabid dog in 1885.

X-rays were developed in 1895.

| 1860s | 1870s | 1880s | 1890s | 1900s |

Louis Pasteur also developed the anthrax vaccine in 1881 and demonstrated its effectiveness by vaccinating sheep.

In 1901, the first Nobel Prize in Physiology or Medicine was awarded to a German physiologist who used antitoxins to create vaccines for diphtheria and tetanus.

That's a Good One!
The Science of Laughter

FIVE different **AREAS** of your **BRAIN** work **TOGETHER** to make you **LAUGH.**

Our bodies physically change when we laugh—
FACIAL muscles stretch, **PULSE** increases, **BLOOD** pressure goes up, and we **BREATHE** faster.

Are You Gelos?

Gelotology is the branch of science devoted to the study of laughter and humor and their effects on the brain and body. It was established in the late 1960s. Gelotology gets its name from the Greek word *gelos*, which means "laughter."

GOOD FOR A LAUGH

Laughter not only helps you cope with stress, but it also lowers certain stress hormones in the body to improve your immune system—which keeps you from getting sick—and improve your overall health.

Laughter for Life

The limbic system plays an important part in laughter. The limbic system is located in the brain and is responsible for many behaviors that are necessary for life, like finding food. This leads scientists to believe that laughter is essential to life!

Can't Laugh This Off

Laughter has a funny effect on the brain! Research has shown that when people hear the sound of laughter, the area of the brain that gets facial muscles ready to move is activated. This explains why it's almost impossible not to smile when you see or hear people laughing!

FROM FUNNY TO FIT

Laughing is good exercise! Research shows that laughing 100 times has the same benefits as 10 minutes on the rowing machine or 15 minutes on an exercise bike.

The Milk Man Louis Pasteur

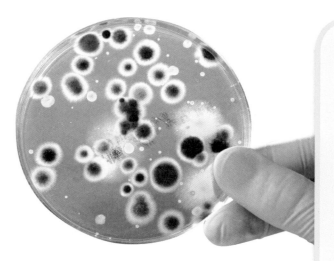

Spoiled Milk

French chemist and microbiologist Louis Pasteur is considered a pioneer of medical microbiology, or the branch of biology that studies microscopic life forms. As a professor at the University of Lille, he was able to show that bacteria caused wine and beer to go bad. Pasteur later demonstrated that milk spoiled the same way. He proved from these experiments that if you boiled and then cooled a liquid, you could remove the bacteria. This technique became known as pasteurization, named after its inventor.

✔ PROVE IT

Pasteur's theories weren't always popular within the scientific community. When he concluded that bacteria didn't spontaneously generate, meaning they didn't come from nowhere, he wasn't initially believed. It wasn't until 1864 that the French Academy of Sciences accepted his research.

Got Silk?

When an epidemic hit the silkworm population in the south of France, Pasteur was asked to investigate. He concluded that the epidemic was caused by parasites, and silkworm eggs that didn't have parasites should be used to make silk. He solved the problem and saved the silk industry.

IN THEORY

Pasteur's work contributed to the germ theory of disease, which stated that infection inside the body is primarily caused by the actions of microscopic organisms. The germ theory of disease was a turning point for modern medicine and spurred the development of vaccines by Pasteur and other scientists.

DID YOU KNOW?

Boo Hoo! Why We Cry

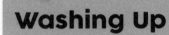

SOME TEARS HAPPEN WITHOUT YOU THINKING ABOUT THEM. THESE TEARS, CALLED REFLEX TEARS, HELP KEEP THE EYES CLEAR OF THINGS THAT IRRITATE THEM, LIKE DUST.

Washing Up

Just as there are different reasons for crying, there are different types of tears. There are tiny glands in the inside corners of the eyes that produce tears, called basal tears, when you blink. These tears clean your eyes and keep them moist, as well as help you to see clearly.

Onion Tears

When you cut an onion, a gas is released which causes a stinging feeling in your eyes when it comes into contact with them. Your eyes form tears to try to dilute, or water down, the gas so you can cry it out!

LAYER UP

DIFFERENT TEARS ARE MADE DIFFERENTLY. THERE ARE THREE LAYERS TO A BASAL TEAR: A **THIN LAYER** ON THE **SURFACE** OF THE EYE, WHICH IS MADE OF **MUCUS**; A **MIDDLE LAYER** THAT IS MORE **WATERY**; AND A **LAYER** THAT IS **OILY** TO PREVENT THE **TEAR** FROM **EVAPORATING.**

It's a Reflex

While both basal and reflex tears have three layers, our reflex tears have more water and more antibodies to keep eyes protected against microorganisms that try to make their way inside.

How Can Eye Stress This?

Emotional tears are the tears we shed in response to emotions. These tears have higher concentrations of stress hormones, which may explain why some people actually feel better after they cry.

Medical Milestones of the 20th Century

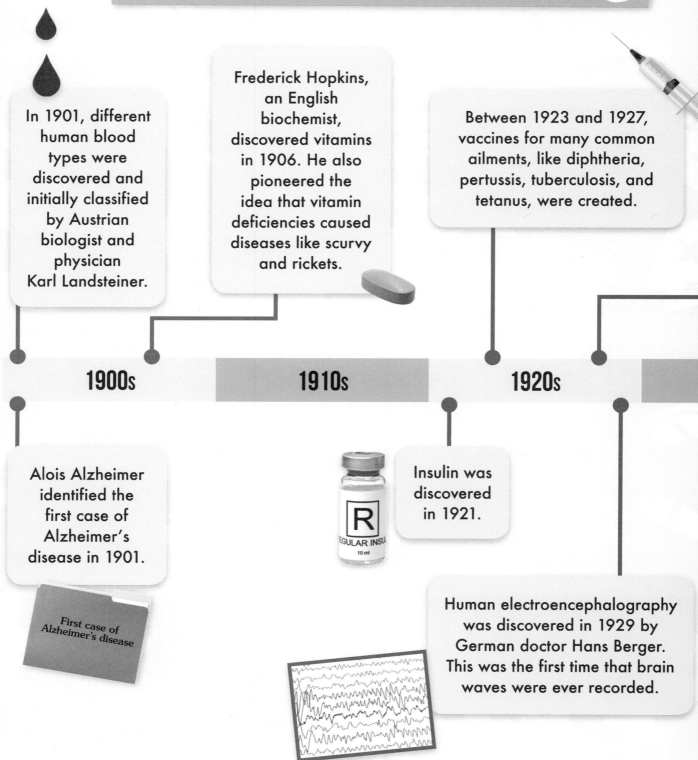

In 1901, different human blood types were discovered and initially classified by Austrian biologist and physician Karl Landsteiner.

Frederick Hopkins, an English biochemist, discovered vitamins in 1906. He also pioneered the idea that vitamin deficiencies caused diseases like scurvy and rickets.

Between 1923 and 1927, vaccines for many common ailments, like diphtheria, pertussis, tuberculosis, and tetanus, were created.

1900s

1910s

1920s

Alois Alzheimer identified the first case of Alzheimer's disease in 1901.

First case of Alzheimer's disease

Insulin was discovered in 1921.

REGULAR INSULIN 10 ml

Human electroencephalography was discovered in 1929 by German doctor Hans Berger. This was the first time that brain waves were ever recorded.

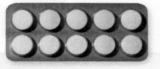

Sir Alexander Fleming discovered penicillin in 1928, saving millions of lives and making a lasting impact on the field of medicine.

In 1960, cardiopulmonary resuscitation (CPR) was invented and successfully tested—on a dog!

1940s　　**1950s**　　**1960s**

Jonas Salk discovered the first polio vaccine in 1952, but the vaccine wasn't made widely available until 1955, following large-scale trials.

The year 1963 saw the first successful transplants of both the human lung and the human liver.

Lungs　　　　Liver

A Product of Our Environment

Where our ancestors lived has had a large impact on how we look and what happens inside our bodies—from our height and weight to our skin color, the composition of our blood, and even our digestive systems!

Fun Fats!

To help balance their diet, which is high in marine mammal fat, Inuit people have special gene mutations—slight changes in their DNA—that help keep their cholesterol under control and reduce the risk of heart disease otherwise increased by a high-fat diet. The mutation also reduces their height.

LIVING THE HIGH LIFE

Groups of people around the world that live high up in the mountains where there is less oxygen in the air have developed different ways of retaining, or holding onto, oxygen. These adaptations include higher concentrations of hemoglobin—the protein in charge of transporting oxygen in the blood—or higher amounts of oxygen in each molecule of hemoglobin.

Working Up a Sweat

In hot, humid climates, humans tend to be taller and leaner to help them dissipate, or get rid of, all the heat they can. Taller bodies have larger surface areas of skin for heat and sweat to dissipate from. Because fat traps heat, leaner bodies are more beneficial in these climates.

No Sweat!

Like people in hot, humid climates, people in hot, dry climates tend to be lean. However, they are generally shorter in order to reduce the amount of water they lose through sweating, since water is so precious in the desert. Shorter people have less surface area from which to sweat, and they require less water, so this adaptation reduces both water loss and amount of water needed.

Pale in Comparison

Early humans living farther from the equator evolved to have lighter skin, because they had less exposure to the sun's UVB rays. Because lighter-skinned people had less access to sunlight, they also evolved to more efficiently process vitamin D so they would be less likely to suffer vitamin D deficiency.

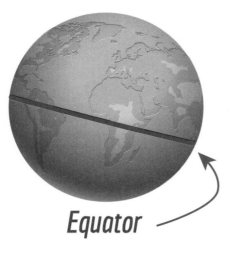

Equator

Don't Go Changing

Because we now have many technological ways to control our environments, like air conditioning, heating, and insulated thermal clothing, there is less reason for us to evolve to better suit the climate outside, so modern human evolution is unlikely to result in changes affected by climate.

The History of Orthopedic Medicine

Close to the Bone

Orthopedic medicine is a special type of medicine that studies the body's skeletal system. To become an orthopedic doctor, a person usually goes through medical school and then completes a special course of study called a residency to focus on orthopedics. An orthopedist can further specialize by becoming a surgeon or by focusing on a particular body part, like the hand or foot.

Bare Bones

Evidence of the study of orthopedics dates back to the Paleolithic period. Bones from that time period have engravings on them that humans made after they ate the meat off of them. It is believed that Hippocrates, an ancient Greek doctor, made splints for broken bones. The skeletal system and muscles were documented in the Roman era.

Part of History

While the first artificial prosthesis—a device used to replace a missing part of the body—is believed to have originated in Roman times, a French doctor named Ambroise Pare is credited with developing amputation techniques, or techniques to remove body parts, as well as techniques for artificial limbs, in the 1500s.

Artificial arm and hand

Artificial leg and foot

X-ray Visionary

X-rays were developed in the mid-1890s when Wilhelm Conrad Roentgen observed (by accident!) that an image made from his cathode ray generator cast passed what was considered the range for cathode rays. He won a Nobel Prize for this discovery.

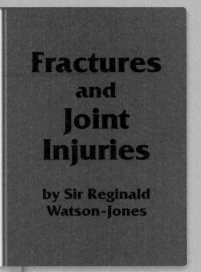

Fractures and Joint Injuries

by Sir Reginald Watson-Jones

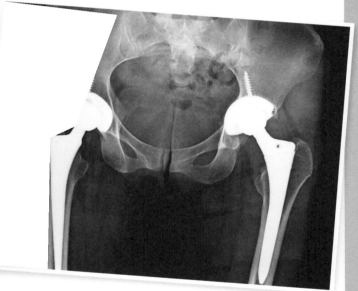

Making Moves

The study of joints and joint replacement also saw great advancement in the 1900s. Dr. Smith-Peterson, a doctor at Harvard University, designed a nail with three prongs that was able to mobilize the hip, or help it move, after it was broken. The first hip arthroplasty, or rebuilding of the hip joint, using metal happened in 1942.

He Wrote the Book

The 1900s saw many important developments in the field of orthopedics. A book called *Fractures and Joint Injuries*, by Sir Reginald Watson-Jones and published in 1940, remained a primary reference for orthopedists for many years. In 1949, stainless steel rods were used to treat bone fractures for the first time, pioneered by H. Lowry Rush.

Medical Milestones of the 21st Century

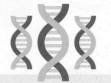

The Human Genome Project, which involved researchers worldwide attempting to sequence and map the 20,000+ genes in human DNA, was completed in 2000.

A special bandage made from the shells of crabs and shrimp, which bond with red blood cells, was developed in 2002 to clot extreme wounds that bleed too much.

2000s

In 2001, the first TeleSurgery was performed: A doctor in New York used a remote-controlled robot to operate on a patient in France.

The 2000s saw a significant decline in smoking rates—and, therefore, smoking-related conditions—thanks to anti-smoking legislation passed in that decade.

The bionic eye was created in 2007.

In 2017, England launched the first trial of 3D printed bionic hands for children. Scientists can use 3D printing to create lighter and more efficient prosthetic limbs. 3D printing is now used for many medical procedures, including bone replacements and hearing aids.

2010s

The first human papillomavirus (HPV) vaccine, Gardasil, was approved in 2006 by the United States Federal Drug Administration (FDA).

The first bionic eye was made available in 2011, after positive trials on completely blind volunteers.

Tendons

MADE TO MOVE

YOU USE TENDONS EVERY TIME YOU MOVE YOUR BODY. TENDONS ARE MADE OF CONNECTIVE TISSUE, WHICH IS TOUGH AND DOESN'T STRETCH. WHEN A MUSCLE CONTRACTS, THE FORCE PRODUCED IS TRANSFERRED TO THE BONES BY THESE FIBROUS TISSUES.

Tend to Your Tendons

Your tendons can become tight, making it harder for them to move and causing you pain. Tendons can become tight from overuse, or doing an activity over and over again using the same tendon, or from incorrect posture over time. Getting older and not stretching can also cause tight tendons.

TENDONS VARY IN **SIZE** AND **SHAPE**, BASED ON WHERE THEY **ARE** IN THE **BODY** AND WHAT THEY **DO. TENDONS** ARE FOUND ALMOST **EVERYWHERE** IN YOUR BODY, INCLUDING YOUR **HANDS, FEET, HEAD, ARMS,** AND **LEGS.**

Tends to Be Tendinitis

Many tendon injuries are considered tendinitis, or inflammation of the tendon. However, a doctor may also diagnose tendinosis, which is a condition defined by small tears in or near the tendon caused by overuse.

Achilles's Heel

The Achilles tendon is the largest and strongest tendon in the body. It connects the muscle of the calf to the bone of the heel and helps you walk and run. Because of the Achilles tendon, you can push off your toes when you move. Achilles injuries are common in athletes and other active people.

DID YOU KNOW?

The Achilles tendon is named after Achilles, a figure in Greek mythology. Greek mythology tells the story of Achilles's mother dipping Achilles by the heel into the River Styx. Because of this, Achilles's heel was the only part of his body that could be injured.

Those Genes Look Good on You: Genetics

The unique blueprint, or design, for how you look and how your body functions is found in your DNA, which is short for deoxyribonucleic acid. DNA is a long, spiral-shaped molecule that is found in every cell in your body.

Manual for Man and Woman

Genes are the pieces of DNA that hold the instructions for making certain proteins. There are about 25,000 genes in the body. Each of these genes is like an instruction booklet or manual for putting you together—one gene is the manual for brown eyes, one gene is the manual for blond hair, one is the manual for how your body makes certain enzymes, and so on!

EARNING YOUR LETTERS

One of the 23 pairs of chromosomes in your body determines your gender. These chromosomes—the X and Y chromosomes—are called sex chromosomes. Females have two of the X chromosomes, and males have an X chromosome and a Y chromosome.

MOM AND DAD GENES

Genes are housed inside chromosomes. Chromosomes are inherited from your parents. Every cell in your body has 46 chromosomes arranged in pairs—half are from your mother, and half are from your father. Human chromosomes can be seen with a high-powered microscope.

Nature and Nurture

Sometimes chromosomes will have a part missing, or have an extra part. In certain cases, a gene is mutated, or changed, in some way. Scientists used to believe that fewer than 3% of diseases were connected to genetic problems, but recent studies have shown ties between genetics and the risk people have for developing many diseases, like diabetes and Parkinson's disease, that weren't originally thought to have any genetic links.

Special Variatio...

Sometimes there...
...in th...
...that happe...

Achoo! The Science of the Sneeze

WHAT IS A SNEEZE?

A sneeze is what happens when your body suddenly forces breath out through your nose and mouth in a noisy way. A sneeze can be caused by anything from sickness, like a cold or flu, to an irritant, like dust, animal dander, pollen, pepper, or perfume.

What happens when you sneeze?

The inside of your nose gets irritated, either by a virus making you sick or an outside source such as pollen. You inhale, and pressure builds in your chest. Your tongue pushes against the top of your mouth. This makes the air you just took in come back out through your nose.

Skip_a_Beat

While the pressure changes that occur in your chest when you sneeze might feel funny, this doesn't mean your heart is stopping. These pressure changes can alter the flow of your blood, which can affect your heart's rhythm, so it feels like your heart momentarily stops—but it's just a change in rhythm!

HIT SNOOZE

SNEEZING IS A REFLEX. WHEN YOU ARE SLEEPING, THE NERVES THAT NEED TO BE ACTIVE FOR YOU TO SNEEZE ARE RELAXED, SO YOU DON'T SNEEZE WHEN YOU SLEEP.

Everybody Poops!

To-do to Doo-doo

Small, hard poop that's difficult to get out is a sign of constipation. Constipation generally happens when there is a lack of fiber in a person's diet. Most people need between 25 and 40 grams of fiber each day. Good sources of fiber are vegetables, fruit, and whole grains.

A POO-R SIGN

Certain medications can turn your poop black or red. If there is blood in your poop, however, it's an indication that something else might be wrong. It could be an ulcer in the stomach or colon, or hemorrhoids, which are the result of swollen veins in and around your rectum.

A Few Poos Loose

Celiac disease can cause poop to be loose, though not necessarily like diarrhea. Celiac disease is often a genetic condition and prevents the body from absorbing gluten, a protein found in wheat, barley, and rye. Gluten is commonly ingested when you eat pasta, bread, cookies, and cakes.

Coming Out on Top

When there's more gas in your intestine than normal, your poop will probably float instead of sink to the bottom of the toilet. While this could indicate a larger problem—like your body's inability to absorb the fat in the food you eat—it usually isn't cause for alarm.

Certain parasites can cause your poop to smell like rotten eggs, while certain infections can cause your poop to be a liquid consistency.

NUMBER 2 PENCIL

If your poop is shaped like a pencil, you may be constipated. If you're plugged up and the muscles can't relax, there's less space for the poop to squeeze through, which makes it longer and thinner than normal.

Surgery and Organ Transplants

Surgical Success

Modern surgery didn't exist before the 1900s, though the 1800s did see improvement in the techniques and protocols—and therefore patient survival rates—of surgery. However, it wasn't until the 1900s that a person had greater than a 50% chance of survival after surgery.

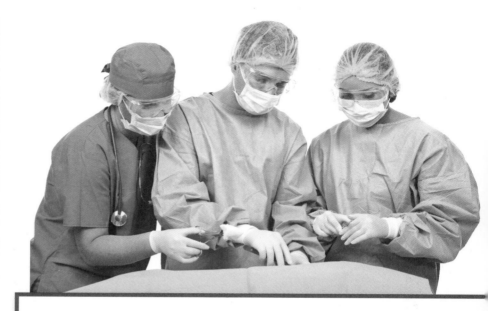

General Education

Some surgeons are considered general surgeons. These surgeons study a wide range of surgical disciplines and related knowledge, including anatomy, pathology, and wound healing. Other fields of surgery include neurological or brain surgery, ophthalmological or eye surgery, orthopedic surgery, and head and neck surgery.

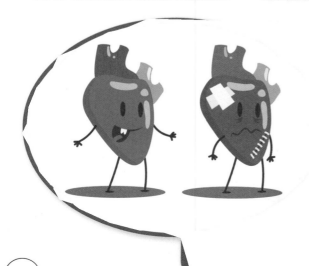

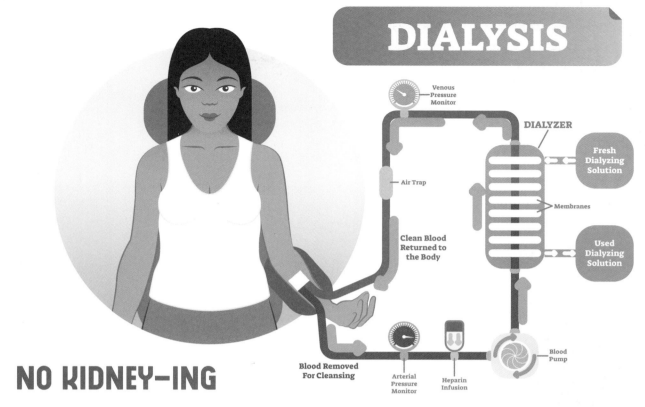

DIALYSIS

Venous Pressure Monitor

DIALYZER

Fresh Dialyzing Solution

Air Trap

Membranes

Clean Blood Returned to the Body

Used Dialyzing Solution

Blood Removed For Cleansing

Arterial Pressure Monitor

Heparin Infusion

Blood Pump

NO KIDNEY-ING

IN 2018, MORE THAN 70,000 PEOPLE WERE WAITING FOR A KIDNEY TRANSPLANT. WHEN A PATIENT HAS KIDNEY FAILURE, HE OR SHE CAN RECEIVE DIALYSIS TREATMENT TO HELP HIS OR HER KIDNEYS FUNCTION UNTIL A DONOR KIDNEY BECOMES AVAILABLE.

DONATION NATION

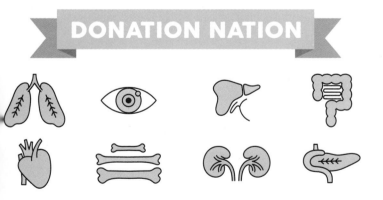

You can donate many organs from your body, including your heart, kidneys, lungs, and liver. There are very strict standards around organ donation, and a national computer system is used to match organs to donors, considering blood types, organ size, and geographic location.

Plastic-Free Surgery

Plastic surgery doesn't involve plastic! It is named after the Greek word *plastikos*, which means "to mold." Plastic surgery is used to change the way a person looks or some aspect of his or her functionality. Reconstructive plastic surgery is used when abnormalities are seen on the face or body as the result of injury or genetics.

Sports Medicine

SPORTS SUPPORT

The field of sports medicine blends together fitness and medicine to prevent and heal sports-related injuries. Sports medicine uses many techniques, including stretching, to help patients avoid injury, or to rehabilitate their bodies when they are injured.

Tackling the Issue

Sports medicine professionals tackle all kinds of injuries sustained during sports or activities. Some of the most common include shin splints, torn rotator cuffs, Achilles tendon issues, and knee problems.

Experience in the Field

A physician specializing in sports medicine focuses on fitness and wellness as a way to prevent injury. Typically, a doctor of sports medicine has a primary medical degree—in family medicine, for example—and undergoes another year or two of training before she or he can be considered a sports medicine physician.

Fit for Consumption

A diet specialist plans meals and diets for athletes, making sure they have the best diets possible to help prevent illness and injury. A diet specialist has to go through a special internship and certification program before he or she can act as a diet specialist for an athlete.

Muscle Memory

People who go into the field of sports medicine often study biomechanics. Biomechanics studies how the principles of physics can be applied to exercise and sports. Biomechanics can help athletes and their sports medicine professionals understand how the muscles, joints, and bones move, providing important information that can help athletes as they work to improve their performance.

Keep Everything Running Smoothly

An exercise physiologist helps assess the effect of exercise, both good and bad, on an athlete's body. The exercise physiologist monitors the athlete's performance and suggests changes if he or she is injured.

191

Systems of the Body
Endocrine System

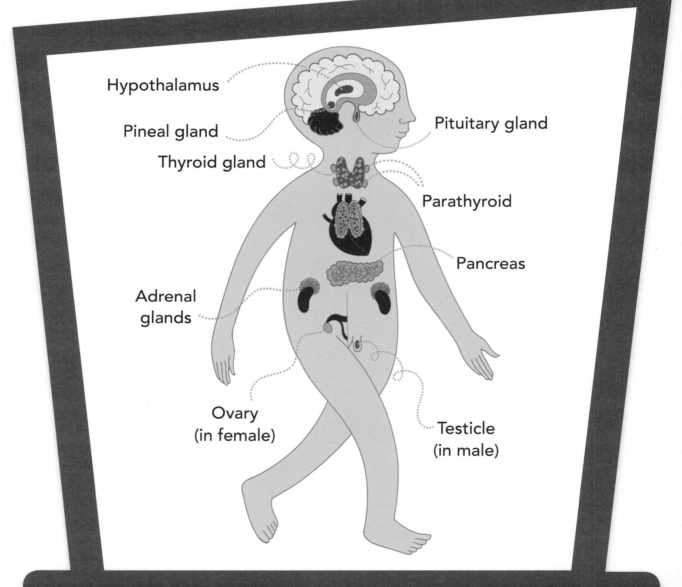

Hypothalamus

Pineal gland

Thyroid gland

Pituitary gland

Parathyroid

Pancreas

Adrenal glands

Ovary (in female)

Testicle (in male)

Keep It Regulated

The body's hormones run the endocrine system. The major glands that make up the endocrine system use hormones as signals that regulate everything from sleep to growth to the body's metabolism. These glands are the pituitary gland, thyroid gland, parathyroid, adrenal glands, pancreas, hypothalamus, pineal gland, and male and female reproductive glands.

We're All Endocr-ine It Together

Glands process materials found in the blood and expel them so the body can use these refined materials somewhere else. Because of this, almost every cell of the body is affected in some way by the endocrine system.

ANCIENT HISTORY

The field of medicine that focuses on the endocrine system is called endocrinology. Even though the use of the word "endocrinology" began in the early 1900s, the actual study of the endocrine system began in ancient China in 200 BC.

GET YOUR DUCTS IN A ROW

Glands are either exocrine or endocrine, meaning they either excrete, or get rid of, materials like hormones through a system of ducts (exocrine), or they excrete hormones into the bloodstream without using ducts (endocrine). The pancreas, a gland of the endocrine system, functions as both endocrine and exocrine, releasing hormones directly into the blood and also into the small intestine through ducts.

HORMONE CRAZY

Problems in the endocrine system are detected when hormone levels are either too high or too low. If your body doesn't respond to hormones in the right way, you might have a hormone disease, but hormone levels can also fluctuate because of stress, infection, or changes in your body's fluids.

THE GLUCOSE LEVEL

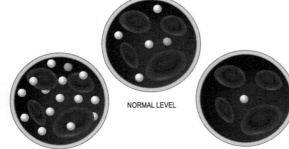

NORMAL LEVEL

HYPERGLYCEMIA
(high blood sugar)

HYPOGLYCEMIA
(low blood sugar)

Not So Sweet

Diabetes is the most common disease of the endocrine system. A diabetic's body can't properly process a simple sugar called glucose. If the body doesn't produce insulin, a hormone usually made in the pancreas that helps process sugar, or use insulin correctly, it will not be able to break down glucose.

Elizabeth Blackwell

Ladies First

Elizabeth Blackwell was born in England on February 3, 1821, but moved to the United States as a child. It was unheard of for women at that time to become doctors, but she ignored criticism and graduated first in her class from medical school, becoming the first female M.D. in the United States.

Making Progress

Blackwell decided to become a doctor after a sick friend told her that she didn't like going to male doctors. Blackwell's friend told her that she felt she would have progressed better had she seen a woman doctor, and that compelled Blackwell to study medicine.

NO KIDDING!

After being rejected by many medical schools, Blackwell was finally accepted into Geneva Medical College in New York. Because women at that time didn't study medicine, the faculty reviewing her application jokingly told the all-male students that a woman had applied to the school, and they would accept her if none of the students objected. The students thought they were playing along with a joke and agreed to her acceptance. She started medical school with her stunned male classmates in November of 1847.

Blackwell really wanted to be a surgeon. After graduating from medical school, she worked in London and in Paris delivering babies. While performing a procedure on an infant, she was infected with a disease that blinded her in one eye and stopped her from continuing a career as a surgeon.

SISTER, SISTER

Blackwell opened two clinics in New York in the mid-1850s, both of which served poor women and children. She opened these clinics with the help of her sister, Emily Blackwell, who followed in her sister's footsteps by becoming a physician and then a surgeon.

Practicing to Get a Practice

Blackwell opened a medical school for women in the late 1860s before going back to London, where she established a private practice and served as a physician and instructor at the London School of Medicine for Women before her death in 1910.

The History of Hospitals

GENEROUS HOSPITAL-ITY

The Roman emperor Constantine the Great is considered to have founded the modern hospital concept. Before this time, hospitals were focused on isolating the patient from his or her community. Constantine, a converted Christian, believed it was the obligation of the members of the community—in this case, the community of Christianity—to care for the ill.

MOBILE MEDICS

Even though the Greeks were said to have been key developers of modern medicine, they didn't have hospitals. Instead, doctors went house to house to see patients. This "house call" model stayed in place for hundreds of years.

DID YOU KNOW?

The word "hospital" originates from the Romans. It is derived from the Latin word *hospes*, meaning "host" or "guest."

New World, Old Hospitals

The oldest hospital in North America was built in 1524 in Mexico City. When the 13 colonies were established, two hospitals were built: Bellevue Hospital in New York, in 1736, and Pennsylvania Hospital in Philadelphia, in 1751.

HOLY HOSPITALS

In the **500s** and 600s, hospitals were formed in **monasteries.** These monasteries had infirmitoria, or **infirmaries,** where sick people received treatment. They also had pharmacies and **gardens** where they grew plants used to make **medicines.**

A Religious Experience

Monasteries pioneered the idea of a hospital ward, where multiple patients were housed at one time. Sometimes, these wards were created to look like crosses, so sick people could see a religious altar. This floor plan started in Florence, Italy, in the 1400s and has continued into modern times—except the center of the ward is now the nurses' station, not an altar!

FUN FACTS about Orthodontics

The wires used in orthodontic appliances, or appliances used to correct the teeth, are thin and flexible and were originally designed by NASA for the space program!

THE FIRST VERSION OF BRACES WAS DESIGNED IN FRANCE IN 1728.

About **4 million** people in the **United States** wear **braces**.

Even mummies wanted straight teeth! Mummies have been found with cords (made from animal intestines!) on their teeth, which archeologists think might have served as an ancient form of braces.

All orthodontists are dentists, but only 6% of dentists are orthodontists.

Even the ancient Greeks had a form of braces—they used metal and the guts of cats to try to improve their smiles.

THERE ARE A LOT OF RUMORS ABOUT BRACES, BUT YOU DON'T HAVE A BETTER CHANCE OF BEING STRUCK BY LIGHTNING IF YOU WEAR THEM, AND THEY WON'T INTERFERE WITH RADIO SIGNALS.

Braces aren't just for kids—1 in 5 orthodontics patients is an adult!

The first certified orthodontist in the United States was Dr. Charles Tweed.

Word Scramble

Dental Terms

Unscramble the letters to find
dental and orthodontic terms.

RCABSE

_ _ _ _ _ _

SMGU

_ _ _ _

YCDAE

_ _ _ _ _

EDROILUF

_ _ _ _ _ _ _ _

EHTET

_ _ _ _ _

NESTIDT

_ _ _ _ _ _ _

TRANIREE

_ _ _ _ _ _ _ _

PLAPICNESA

_ _ _ _ _ _ _ _ _ _

THORDISTONOT

_ _ _ _ _ _ _ _ _ _ _ _

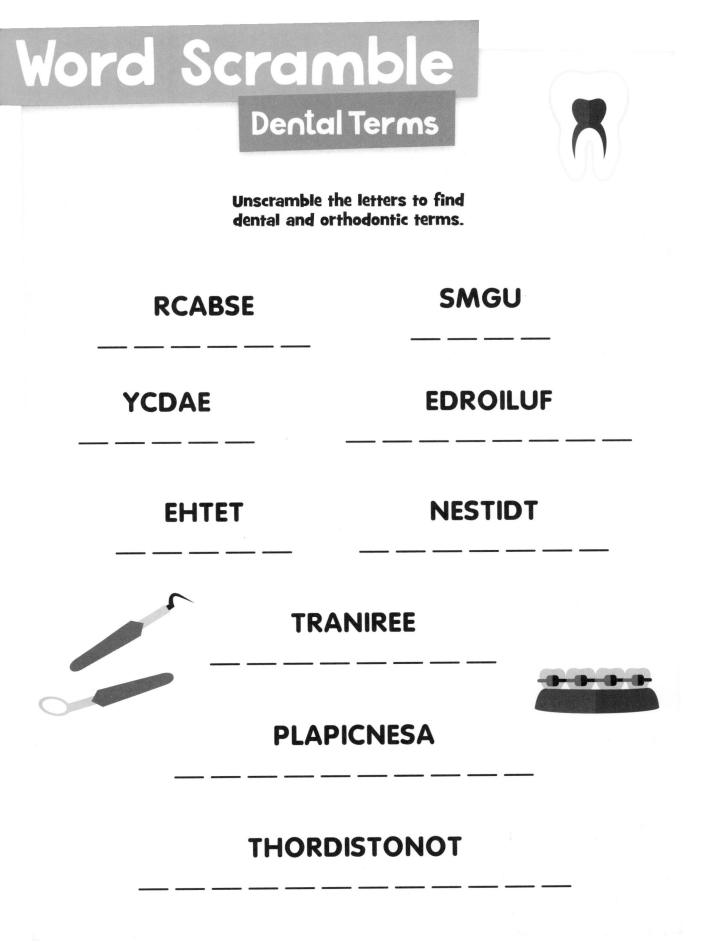

Bone Marrow

BONE ANATOMY

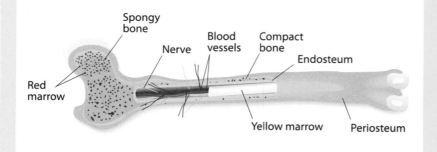

Spongy bone

Nerve

Blood vessels

Compact bone

Endosteum

Red marrow

Yellow marrow

Periosteum

Blood and Bones

There are two types of bone marrow that fill the medullary cavities, or centers of bones: red bone marrow, called myeloid tissue, and yellow bone marrow, called fatty tissue. The job of red bone marrow is to make new blood cells—about 200 billion every day!

Building To-marrow's Cells

Stem cells are immature cells, which become other cells in the body. The bone marrow houses two different kinds of stem cells—mesenchymal and hematopoietic. Hematopoietic stem cells are found in red bone marrow and form blood, and mesenchymal stem cells are found in yellow bone marrow and make bone, fat, and cartilage.

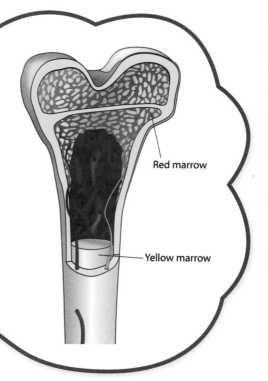

Red marrow

Yellow marrow

Busy Baby Bones

Bone marrow is considered active if it is still making new marrow cells. Newborn babies have active marrow, but by the time a person is a young adult, the arm, leg, hand, and foot bones have stopped making new marrow. Active marrow in adults is found in the skull, ribs, breastbone, spine, hip, and shoulder.

Narrow on Marrow?

If a person's bone marrow doesn't make enough blood cells, he or she may need a bone marrow transplant. In a transplant, damaged marrow is replaced with healthy marrow cells. These new blood stem cells can come from the patient's body or from a donor. A doctor can extract the bone marrow with a needle, take the cells directly from the patient or the donor's blood, or take the cells from the blood found in the umbilical cord of a newborn baby.

Normal blood   Leukemia

BAD TO THE BONE

LEUKEMIA IS A TYPE OF CANCER THAT STARTS IN THE BONE MARROW, EVEN THOUGH IT'S REALLY A DISEASE OF THE BLOOD. IF SOMEONE HAS LEUKEMIA, HIS OR HER WHITE BLOOD CELLS KEEP MULTIPLYING, WHICH CAUSES ISSUES WITH THE NORMAL PRODUCTION OF WHITE AND RED BLOOD CELLS.

Family Bone-ding

If transplanted cells come from the patient's own body, it's called an autologous transplant. If the cells come from an identical sibling, it's a syngeneic transplant, and if they come from a donor, it's an allogeneic transplant. While members of the patient's family often provide the best match, there are donor registries where people can volunteer to donate their marrow to a patient with whom they match. A match is made when two people have white blood cells with the same kind of protein, called a human leukocyte antigen (HLA).

The Bladder

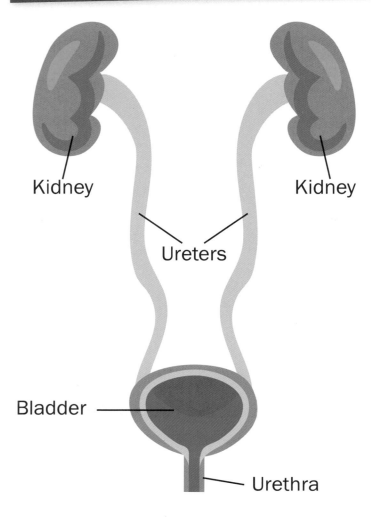

Kidney

Kidney

Ureters

Bladder

Urethra

AS MUCH AS WEE CAN

Your bladder can expand and contract depending on the amount of liquid inside. The bladder can comfortably hold nearly 16 ounces—almost half the size of a liter bottle of soda—for up to five hours! When empty, it shrinks back to its normal size.

BLADDER MATTER

The bladder and the kidneys are connected by ureters, which are two long tubes that transport urine from where it is made in the kidneys to the bladder. Inside the bladder are four layers of tissue, muscle, blood vessels, and fat.

EITHER URINE OR UR-OUT

Your bladder has one main function: to hold your urine and then pee it out! The bladder is an organ the size of a grapefruit that stores urine in an area located behind the pelvic bone and below the kidneys.

Let It Go

Sometimes you have to hold your pee, but it's a good idea not to wait to go—"holding it" isn't good for your bladder. Repeatedly holding your urine can cause your bladder to expand too much, which can put pressure on the kidneys and cause you to not be able to fully empty your bladder.

ON A PEE SPREE

One of the most common bladder conditions is an overactive bladder. An overactive bladder can be caused by anything from too much caffeine to a bladder infection.

The bladder opening is connected to the urethra. At this opening sits a small, circular muscle called a sphincter—when this muscle contracts, no urine can leak out. When you pee, the detrusor muscle squeezes and the sphincter releases, causing urine to flow through the urethra and out of the body.

Everybody Pees!

IN THE CLEAR

Completely clear pee means you are drinking enough water—maybe even too much! In certain cases, overhydration can lead to health problems, but it's rare. A good color for urine is light yellow—almost the color of honey—which means you are hydrated. Make sure you drink more fluids if the color starts to darken.

TRUE COLORS

Most of the time, changes in the color of your urine have to do with hydration: The colors, from clear to dark, reflect how much fluid you are taking in versus how much you are putting out. Sometimes, however, the color changes indicate something wrong with a certain organ. Red could indicate blood in the urine and a problem with your kidneys, while a brownish color could mean an issue with your liver.

You Don't Want These CRYSTALS

If urine crystallizes in the bladder, stones will form. These hard urine crystals make it difficult for a person to empty his or her bladder and can be very painful.

Pink Pee?

Pink or red urine can be caused by something you ate–like beets–but other medical conditions may also cause the red tint, and in those cases, the color change is due to blood in your urine. A doctor will take a culture, or sample, of your urine and analyze it to see what might be causing the color to change.

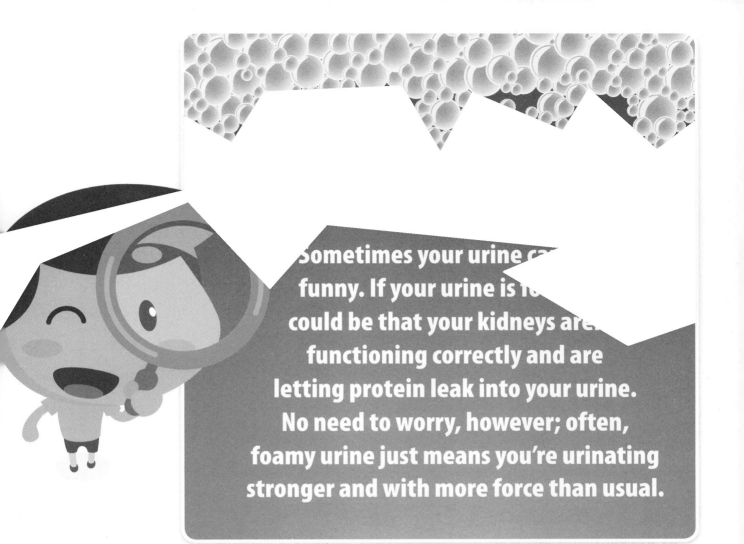

Sometimes your urine ca... funny. If your urine is fo... could be that your kidneys are... functioning correctly and are letting protein leak into your urine. No need to worry, however; often, foamy urine just means you're urinating stronger and with more force than usual.

URINE TROUBLE IF YOU EAT THIS

Certain foods can cause your pee to smell funny. Asparagus, for example, can cause your urine to smell different just 15 minutes after you eat it. This is because our bodies break down asparagusic acid—which, as far as scientists know, is only found in asparagus— into a group of compounds that contain sulfur. Substances and foods that contain sulfur, like garlic, usually don't smell great. When your body changes asparagusic acid into a sulfur-rich compound, it vaporizes into the air and up to your nose when you urinate, creating a weird smell.

Animal Instincts

Differences Between Humans and Other Animals

You Heard It Here

Even though a katydid's ears are on its legs, they are remarkably like our ears! Katydids and humans have similar mechanics in their ears that amplify vibrations and send information to their nervous systems. While katydid ears aren't as sophisticated as human ears, they can hear sounds at a higher range.

Mirror, Mirror

Like humans, certain animals can recognize their reflections when they are in front of mirrors. If they see something unusual with their reflections, all great apes, dolphins, elephants, and magpies will try to remove it.

BONE TO PICK

The skeletons of humans and other animals are different. Human skulls are oriented vertically—that is, our faces go up and down, while most animal faces are oriented horizontally, or side-to-side. The mouths of humans differ from the mouths of other animals, too, specifically in the size and shape of their teeth.

_ar skull

Tough Competition

Many animals swim and run faster than humans; other species can fly; and an eagle's vision is eight times clearer than a human's vision. However, no animal can outrun a human when it comes to long distance. Yiannis Kouros, a legendary ultramarathoner, once ran 160 kilometers (nearly 100 miles) in under 12 hours!

Something Smells

Some animal species, like dogs and sharks, have stronger senses of smell than humans. Animals use the sense of smell and other senses to gather information about the world around them. Insects like flies, for example, have taste sensors on their feet so they can taste anything they land on. Other animals have even more impressive sense organs: Birds and bees can see ultraviolet light; snakes can detect infrared light; and bats and dolphins can interpret sonar sounds.

Hey, Bird Brain!

Differences Between Human Brains and Other Animal Brains

Baby Brain

Human babies' brains are very underdeveloped compared to those of other primate babies. That's why human babies are completely dependent on their caregivers when they are born, while other primate babies don't rely nearly as much on their caregivers. In fact, a human would have to be pregnant for 18 to 21 months instead of the usual nine months to produce a baby born with a brain as developed as a newborn chimpanzee!

ONLY HUMAN

Researchers have seen some of the components for human cognition, or the process of thinking and knowing—like those that make up our ability to have abstract thoughts—in other species but not at the same level as what is seen in humans. Scientists still don't know why the human brain evolved to have such high levels of cognitive abilities, while the brains of other animal species did not.

IT'S IN THE DNA

Genetically speaking, humans are very similar to other animals. Humans and the animals we are most like—including chimpanzees, bonobos, and gorillas—share more than 90% of the same DNA.

Up Front

The main difference between a human brain and another animal brain is its size. The frontal lobes of human brains are larger than the frontal lobes of other animals. The frontal lobe controls functions like logic and abstract thought—functions we view as more complicated than what any other animal can perform.

Frontal lobe

Recent studies have shown that the brains of dogs, like humans, can not only make sense of vocal sounds—like dogs barking or humans talking—but they can understand their emotional undertones. In one study, scientists trained dogs to lie still in an MRI machine while they played recordings of dogs and humans making emotional noises—laughing, crying, playful barking, and whining, among other sounds. The dogs not only responded to the sounds, but they responded to the emotional tone of the sounds.

Battle of the Sexes

Differences Between Males and Females

THAT'S DEEP

Generally speaking, men have deeper voices than women. This is because men have more of a hormone called testosterone than women, causing the pitch of their voices to be lower. They also have bigger voice boxes, which are surrounded by bigger pieces of cartilage than the cartilage that surrounds a woman's voice box. This causes men to have larger Adam's apples, too!

MAKING CONNECTIONS

In both males and females, logical thinking happens in the left side of the brain, while intuition happens in the right side. Because women have more connections going from left to right across the brain, they may be able to connect information and draw conclusions better than men. Men, however, tend to have stronger motor and spatial skills, and sometimes have better perception of what's going on around them, because of the greater number of front-to-back connections in their brains.

Big-boned

Men tend to have longer fingers and bigger hands than women, because their bones are bigger. The same goes for the arm bones and leg bones: Male limb bones are thicker and longer than those of women.

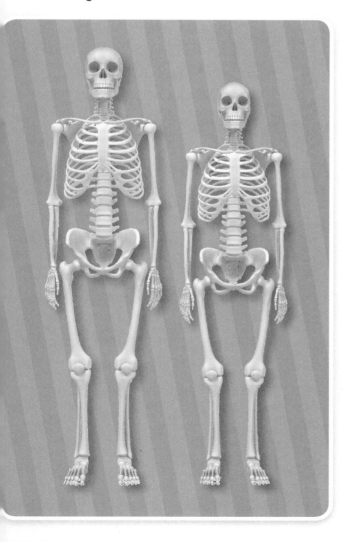

A male brain tends to be about **10% larger** than a female brain. That **doesn't** mean men are smarter: A study of more than **40,000 brain scans** showed **no correlation** between the **size** of someone's brain and his or her **intelligence.**

Is This Boring You?
I'm Yawning

Be-yawned Our Knowledge

Humans yawn, as do most vertebrates, or animals with spines. The reason why, however, is still a mystery to science. There are several theories, some suggesting there is a need for our bodies to yawn, and others suggesting it's purely an involuntary, social reaction.

Starting Yawn-g

As early as the first trimester of pregnancy, a baby inside its mother's womb will yawn. We continue to yawn all throughout our lives, unless something happens to us neurologically.

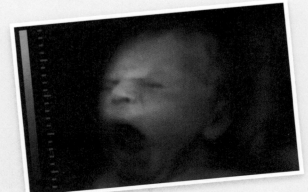

YAWN TIME

One theory about why we yawn ties the most common times people yawn—when they are tired, bored, or hungry—to the reason we yawn. According to this theory, a yawn is a signal to our body that it needs to stay alert!

CATCHING YAWN

Like laughing, yawning is contagious! People also spontaneously yawn when they think about yawning. According to one study, nearly 80% of people asked to think about yawning, yawned!

IT'S YAWN-IVERSAL

Why yawns are contagious, or spread from person to person, is even more of a mystery than yawning itself. Some scientists believe yawning is the body showing empathy, or sharing the feelings of others. While humans aren't the only animals that yawn, humans are the only animals to experience contagious yawns. What's more, contagious yawning develops after age five—about the time empathy starts to develop.

COOL IT

Another yawn theory suggests yawning is designed to cool the brain. The stretch you feel in your jaw when you yawn increases the blood going to your head, and when you breathe in, that breath forces blood and spinal fluid down, away from the brain. That air cools these fluids, which can flow back into the brain.

The History of Exercise

Ancient Times

ANCIENT CHINESE SECRET

In ancient China, the philosopher Confucius taught the importance of physical activity. At this time, people began to recognize that certain diseases—like heart disease, though it wasn't called that at the time—could be avoided with exercise. People in ancient China participated in gymnastics, wrestling, dancing, and archery to stay fit.

ON THE HUNT

HUMANS HAVE BEEN EXERCISING SINCE PREHISTORIC TIMES. PRIMITIVE PEOPLE WOULD GO ON HUNTING AND GATHERING EXPEDITIONS THAT MIGHT LAST UP TO TWO DAYS. AFTER A SUCCESSFUL HUNT, PREHISTORIC PEOPLE WOULD PARTICIPATE IN CELEBRATIONS THAT INCLUDED WALKING UP TO 20 MILES TO NEIGHBORING VILLAGES FOR DANCING AND GAMES.

IT'S ALL GREEK

Ancient Greek civilization focused heavily on physical fitness. Young boys in Athens started an intense fitness program at a young age, mostly doing gymnastics. When they reached adulthood, which was considered to be between the ages of 14 and 16, the fitness program was moved to a gymnasium. There, the young men were supervised by the *paidotribe,* who served as a personal trainer. Here they practiced gymnastics, running, jumping, and wrestling.

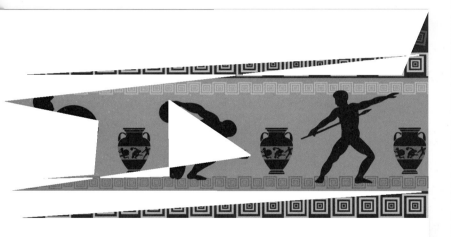

Namaste!

People have been practicing yoga for the past 5,000 years. Yoga, which literally means "union," began in India. While nobody knows the exact story of its origin, Hatha yoga—which is the type of yoga people are most familiar with today—was developed by Hindu priests who copied the movements of animals, hoping to find the same kind of balance with nature that they observed in animals.

SPARTA THE ROUTINE

The ancient civilization of Sparta, located in northern Greece, thought even more highly of fitness than the ancient Athenians. The Spartans were a warring people, and they kept physically fit so they could be prepared for war. Boys started a fitness routine at age six. From that point on, they were required to stay fit and strong so they could serve in the military. Girls were also required to stay fit so they could produce offspring, or children, who could serve in the military in the future.

215

Fill in the Blanks

Exercise in Ancient Times

**Fill in the missing letters to complete the facts below.
For help, look at the previous pages about the history of exercise.**

Prehistoric people found their food by __ H __ __ __ __ N __
and __ __ A __ __ E __ __ __ G.

This Chinese philosopher, __ __ O __ __ __ C __ __ __,
encouraged physical fitness to increase health.

This was the ancient Greek version of a physical trainer:
__ __ __ D __ __ R __ __ __.

The ancient Greek civilization of __ __ P __ __ T __
highly valued physical fitness in both men and women.

Yoga literally translates to this word: __ __ __ I __ N.

Multiple ancient civilizations enjoyed practicing and
playing the same sports, like: W __ __ S __ L __ __ __
and __ __ M __ __ T __ S.

The goal of yoga is to achieve __ __ __ A __ C __ with nature.

Answers on page 312

Dietitians and nutritionists study food and the science of nutrition. They help people determine what to eat so they can live as healthily as possible. The patients they work with include people with food allergies, diseases, or weight concerns.

Meeting Their Needs

In order to help patients achieve their goals, dietitians and nutritionists meet with them to assess their health concerns and needs. They may discuss healthy eating habits and develop meal plans for patients, or they may work with patients to manage specific diseases, such as diabetes, with their diets.

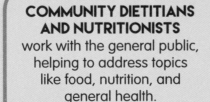

DIFFERENT TYPES OF DIETITIANS AND NUTRITIONISTS

CLINICAL DIETITIANS AND NUTRITIONISTS, who provide nutrition therapy specific to a certain disease, such as kidney disease, usually work in a clinical setting, like a hospital or a nursing home.

COMMUNITY DIETITIANS AND NUTRITIONISTS work with the general public, helping to address topics like food, nutrition, and general health.

MANAGEMENT DIETITIANS work in food service in places like hospitals and schools. They plan food programs and sometimes handle things like managing the kitchen staff or buying food.

FUN FACTS

Names of Bones

Of the more than 200 bones in the human body, half are found in the hands and feet. Here are some of the many types of bones in the body.

Cranial bones are bones of the head and include frontal, parietal, temporal, occipital, sphenoid, and ethmoid.

The ear bones include the malleus, incus, and stapes.

The thorax bones include the sternum and ribs.

The bones of the upper and lower arm include the humerus, radius, and ulna.

The bones of the pelvis include the sacrum, coccyx, and hip bone.

The bones of the leg include the thighbone, or femur, patella, tibia, and fibula.

The bones of the hand and wrist include the scaphoid, lunate, triquetral, pisiform, trapezium, trapezoid, capitate, and hamate bones of the wrist; the metacarpals in the palm; and the phalanges–proximal, intermediate, and distal–of the fingers.

The bones of the feet and ankle include: the calcaneus bone of the heel; talus, navicular, medial cuneiform, intermediate cuneiform, lateral cuneiform, cuboid, and metatarsals of the ankle; and the phalanges—proximal, intermediate, and distal—of the toes.

Gems for the Body
Minerals

Minerals in the body are similar to vitamins, because they also assist with the healthy growth and development of the body. Minerals build strength in the bones, transmit nerve impulses, make hormones, and even keep your heartbeat regular.

IRON, MAN

Iron is important, because it helps move oxygen around your body. Iron is necessary to make hemoglobin, which is the part of the red blood cell that transports oxygen throughout the body. Iron is found in red meat, salmon, eggs, dried fruits, leafy green vegetables, and whole grains.

GETTING IN ZINC

YOUR IMMUNE SYSTEM NEEDS ZINC TO HELP FIGHT ILLNESS AND INFECTION. ZINC CAN HELP WITH THE HEALING PROCESS, SUCH AS AFTER YOU GET A CUT. ZINC-RICH FOODS INCLUDE BEEF AND PORK, NUTS, AND LEGUMES.

nimal, Vegetable, or Mineral?

ou can get most of the
minerals your body needs from
food. Calcium, for example,
comes from dairy products,
leafy green vegetables, and
foods like orange juice or cereal
fortified with calcium, which
means calcium has been added
to that food. Calcium is an
important mineral for building
and keeping your bones strong
and healthy.

Go Bananas

Potassium is necessary to sustain your muscles
and to keep your nervous system properly
working. Bananas are particularly rich in
potassium, as are tomatoes, citrus fruits, low-fat
milk products, and legumes like beans and lentils.

This Joint Is Jumpin'

Your bones meet at your joints, and a bone can have more than one joint. Joints allow you to move, and they are what makes it possible for a dancer to dance gracefully and an athlete to run smoothly. Two Greek words—*arthros*, which means "joint," and *logos*, which means "to study"—combine to create the term for the study of joints: "arthrology."

THE RIGHT CONNECTIONS

There are three main types of joints, named for the kind of material that connects that particular joint with another. The classifications of joints are fibrous, cartilaginous, and synovial. As the name suggests, fibrous tissue connects fibrous joints. Cartilage, or a mix of cartilage and tissue, joins together cartilaginous joints, and synovial joints have a capsule filled with synovial fluid around the joint.

A JOINT EFFORT

Your joints and your bones work together to keep you stable and upright. Without your joints, your bones would experience a great deal of friction and impact whenever you moved. In addition to helping with the body's movement, joints also give you room to grow. The joints in your knees and elbows allow your limbs to grow, and the sutures in your skull, or the places where your skull bones meet, expand to accommodate brain growth.

Can't Leave This Joint

Most fibrous joints are connected by strong, short fibrous tissue. Because the amount of movement these joints allow depends on the length of the fibrous tissue that connects to your bones, fibrous joints don't move very much.

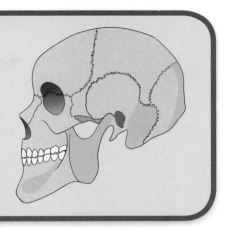

The Not-So-Distant Suture

The sutures in your skull are fibrous joints. In newborn babies, these sutures aren't completely connected. Babies have a soft spot where the sutures aren't joined, called a fontanelle. As the skull grows, the soft spot is replaced by bone, and that soft spot turns into a suture. By the time you are out of your teenage years, your skull bones will be fully fused, or connected, and the skull sutures fully closed.

DID YOU KNOW?

Cartilaginous joints are considered either primary or secondary. When you are young, your primary cartilaginous joints—like in your knee—are connected by cartilage. Later, that cartilage will turn into bone. The joints in your spine are secondary cartilaginous joints. This means fibrous tissue connects them, and their ends are covered with cartilage.

The Ability of Mobility

There are six types of synovial joints, each allowing for a different type of movement. For example, there is a plane joint in your shoulder, between your shoulder blade and your collarbone. Bones connected to plane joints are usually flat so the joint can allow for a sliding type of movement.

Elbows Hinge on This

When a synovial joint, like your elbow joint, moves at a right angle, it's called a hinge joint. At the elbow, this type of joint connects the arm bones of the humerus and the ulna. Because of hinge joints, you can bend and flex, or extend and straighten, your elbow.

'S ALL IN THE WRIST

The condyloid joint is a type of synovial joint found in your

in two axes, allowing your

move side to side, and rotate.

On Rotation

Pivot joints are synovial joints that only rotate. You can rotate your head because you have pivot joints in your neck. In these joints, one bone acts like a ring, and the other bone has a rounded piece that rotates inside that ring.

Keep the Ball Rolling

The ball-and-socket joints are well-known synovial joints, likely because they are the most functional. They get their name from the fact that one joint has a socket, and the other joint is a ball resting in that socket. Along with your shoulder joints, your hip joints are ball-and-socket joints. Ball-and-socket joints are multi-axial, meaning they move in many axial planes, and can bend and flex, open and close, rotate, and move in circles.

SADDLE UP

Like condyloid joints, saddle joints can move in two axes. This joint gets its name from the fact that the bones it connects look like a saddle—one surface is convex, or curved out, and one is concave, or curved inward. The joint at the base of your thumb is a saddle joint.

Kneed to Know

It's Complicated

Your knee is one complicated joint! Because it is made up of bone, ligament, and cartilage, injury to any part of the knee can have a lasting impact on how you move. The thighbone, or femur, meets the fibula and tibia, which are the bones below the knee, at the knee joint. Strong yet flexible ligaments in the knee help stabilize it and allow you to walk or run.

A Crucial Ligament

One of the most commonly injured ligaments in sports is the anterior cruciate ligament (ACL). The ACL helps keep your legs from buckling and keeps your feet under your knees. It guides the shinbone, so if you perform a sudden move, like twisting or bending during sports, you could tear or damage the ligament.

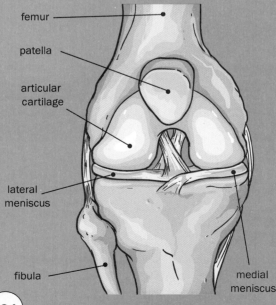

femur
patella
articular cartilage
lateral meniscus
fibula
medial meniscus

A CUSHY JOB

THE CARTILAGE IN THE **KNEE** IS CALLED THE **MENISCUS**, SOMETIMES REFERRED TO IN THE PLURAL, **MENISCI**. THESE STRUCTURES SIT BETWEEN THE BOTTOM OF THE **FEMUR** AND THE TOP OF THE **TIBIA**. THE JOB OF THE **MENISCI** IS TO CUSHION THE **KNEE JOINT**.

Extra Padding

Bursae are small sacs filled with fluid designed to provide cushioning between bones and other body parts, including tendons, muscles, and skin. Bursae help reduce friction and allow smooth movement of the body.

Bursae of the knee

- Suprapatellar bursa
- Prepatellar bursa
- Deep and superficial infrapatellar bursa

NEW KNEE

If you've injured your knee and are having trouble doing everyday things like walking, you might need knee replacement surgery, even if you've tried other treatments. This type of surgery is very common; doctors in the United States perform more than 600,000 knee replacements every year. Knee replacement surgery is also referred to as arthroplasty, which means the surgery of a joint such as the knee or hip.

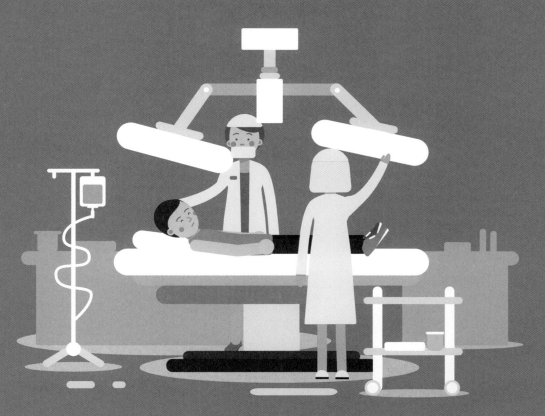

Shoulder Joints

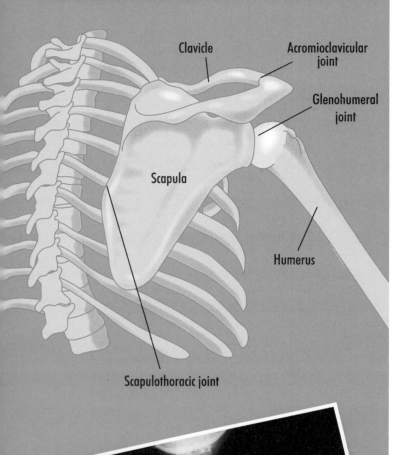

Clavicle

Acromioclavicular joint

Glenohumeral joint

Scapula

Humerus

Scapulothoracic joint

Your shoulder is made up of many layers, including the clavicle, or collarbone, and the shoulder blade, known as the scapula. In most people, you can identify these bones from outside the body, because they jut out and form arches from which your arms hang.

ON THE BALL

The shoulder joint is a ball-and-socket joint. It is stabilized by ligaments, but only loosely. Because of this, your shoulder joint is more flexible than other joints, but it also means it can be pulled out of its socket—or dislocated—more easily than other joints.

Against the Collar

The collarbone is the only shoulder bone that directly attaches to your ribcage, and it supports the weight of your entire arm. If your collarbone breaks, your shoulder will sag.

Tendinitis and Bursitis

You will feel pain if you inflame or irritate the shoulder tendon, causing tendinitis. Baseball pitchers and swimmers often suffer from this kind of tendinitis. Bursitis happens when there is irritation of bursae, which is usually caused by performing a repetitive motion, like throwing.

Worn Out

If you use your rotator cuff extensively, you can wear it out, resulting in a tear. Painters, carpenters, tennis players, and baseball players injure their shoulders this way because of overuse. Sometimes the tear can be healed with physical therapy and medication, or it may require surgery.

Off the Cuff

Your rotator cuffs protect your shoulder joints and help you raise and rotate your arms. The muscles and tendons of each rotator cuff keep the head of the arm bone—the "ball"—in the shoulder socket. There are four rotator cuff muscles, each with its own role and purpose: supraspinatus, which helps lift your arm; infraspinatus, which rotates and extends your shoulder; teres minor, which rotates the arm away from the body; and subscapularis, which helps you lower your arm and hold it straight.

Kidney Stones

Set in Stone

Kidney stones are formed from chemicals that are normally dissolved in urine. If there is more waste than liquid, crystals will form. They will continue to grow unless the stones are expelled from the body when a person pees.

Kidney stones

FEELING STUCK

Most people have enough liquid in their bodies to clean out chemicals without stones forming. In some people, stones will form that are small enough to pass through the body without causing any pain. If the stones can't get out, and they cause urine to back up somewhere in the urinary system, a person will feel a lot of pain.

Family Stones

If you don't drink enough water, or you exercise too much or too little, you may be at a higher risk for kidney stones. Other risk factors include obesity and even eating too much very salty or sugary food. Family history plays a big role in kidney stones as well. If someone in your family is prone to kidney stones, you may be, too.

Genetic

Not drinking enough fluids

Overweight

Foods

Kidney Stones

**Complete the crossword using the clues below.
For help, look at the opposite page.**

ACROSS

2. To help prevent kidney stones, avoid eating too much food with sugar or ____

5. This is one risk factor for kidney stones

8. You need to drink enough of this to help avoid kidney stones

9. Large kidney stones can cause a person to feel this

DOWN

1. If a ____ member has kidney stones, you may be more likely to get them

3. Small kidney stones leave the body in this

4. Tiny crystals that are made of more waste than liquid

6. What kidney stones will do if they aren't removed from the body

7. Stones cause backups in this system of the body

FUN FACTS about
Muscles

There are three types of muscle:

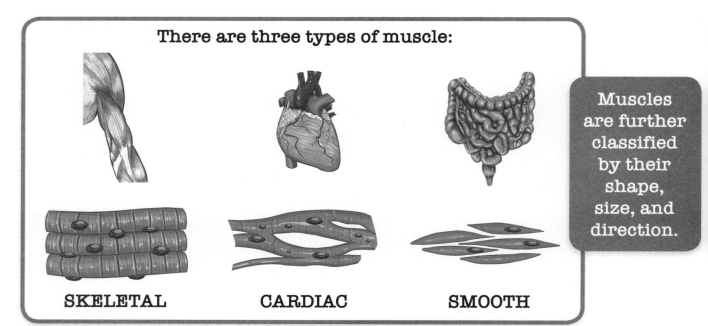

SKELETAL   CARDIAC   SMOOTH

Muscles are further classified by their shape, size, and direction.

Because the muscles in your heart and digestive system are involuntary, you never have to think about beating your heart or digesting your food!

Muscle tissue is denser than fatty tissue.

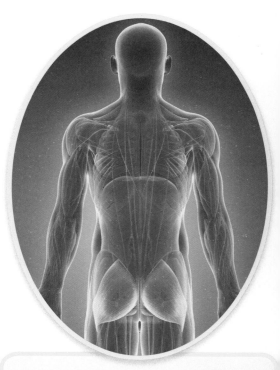

The gluteus maximus, or the butt muscle, is the largest muscle.

About 85% of the total heat produced inside the body comes from muscle movement.

Your **TONGUE** is one of the **STRONGEST** muscles in your body.

Muscle makes up around half of a human's total body weight.

Cardiac muscle is only found in the heart and is the only muscle in the muscular system that never gets tired.

It takes longer to lose muscle than to gain it.

THE CALF MUSCLE EXERTS THE MOST FORCE OF ANY MUSCLE.

Muscles grow while you sleep. In the deepest stages of sleep, blood flow increases, and the hormones needed for muscle development repair muscles and fuel their growth.

Spinal Cord

Running through the spinal canal, from the base of your brain to your lower back, is your spinal cord. This incredibly important part of the body is actually a group of nerves that allows the brain and body to communicate. Messages from the brain and the nerves move up and down the spinal cord.

VERTEBRA

Pia matter
Arachnoid
Dura matter

White matter
Gray matter

Spinal Nerve
Body of Vertebra
Bone of Vertebra

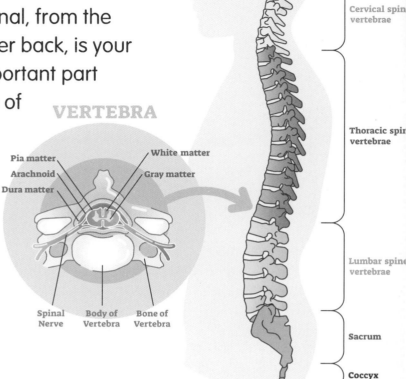

Cervical spin vertebrae

Thoracic spin vertebrae

Lumbar spine vertebrae

Sacrum

Coccyx

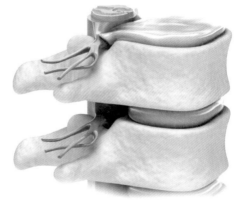

VARIOUS VERTEBRAE

The vertebrae of your spine are protected by discs, which allow the spine to be flexible. There are 24 bones in your vertebrae—seven cervical vertebrae, 12 thoracic vertebrae, and five lumbar vertebrae.

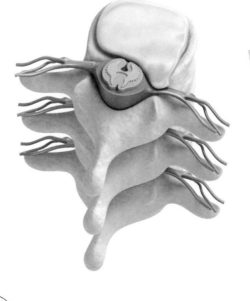

DID YOU KNOW?

The spinal cord has more than 100 joints, 220 ligaments, and 120 muscles. These joints, ligaments, and muscles work together to create an incredibly strong body part. It would require a force greater than 3,000 newtons to fracture the cervical spine——equal to the impact created by a 500-pound car crashing into a wall at 30 miles per hour!

Strike a Cord

The spinal cord isn't very thick. It is only about 1 centimeter around. Your spinal cord stops growing once you pass the age of five. However, it is very flexible: If you took your spinal cord out of your body and bent it, it could make about two-thirds of a circle!

Puberty

Between the ages of eight and 13 in girls and nine and 15 in boys, your body will start to change from a kid's body to an adult's body. During puberty, your body grows faster than it will at any other point in life, except for when you were a baby.

70

60

50

40

30

20

10

PITUITARY PARTY

When puberty begins, the pituitary gland in both boys and girls releases hormones. This gland, located at the bottom of the brain, sends out different hormones depending on if you are a boy or a girl. Boys produce testosterone, while girls produce estrogen.

PITUITARY GLAND

Hypothalamic neurons

Hypothalamus

In-flowing blood

Secretory cells of adenohypophosis

Arteries

In-flowing blood

Anterior pituitary

Posterior pituitary

Veins

Hormones

Brain

Splitting Hairs

One of the **telltale signs** of puberty is new **hair growth.** Both **boys** and **girls** will begin to grow body hair. This hair is thin to start, but will become **thicker, curlier, and darker** throughout **puberty.** Boys also will start to grow **facial hair.**

Working Overtime

Puberty hormones cause the glands in your skin to go into overtime. This means your sweat glands start producing more sweat. Sweat, together with the bacteria on your skin, can cause body odor.

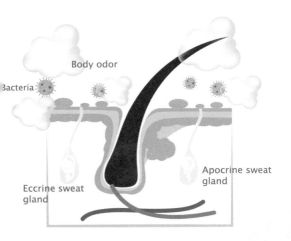

Body odor

Bacteria

Apocrine sweat gland

Eccrine sweat gland

Deodorant

Reproductive System
Male

The male reproductive system includes the **testicles**, a **duct system**, accessory glands like the **prostate**, and the **penis**.

Testicles are part of both the **reproductive system** and the **endocrine system**, since they are responsible for producing hormones, like **testosterone**.

The **male reproductive system** is located **inside** and **outside** the pelvis.

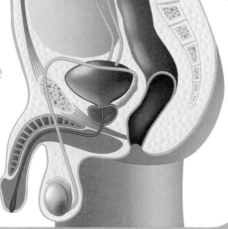

Boys are not able to physically reproduce until puberty, even though a boy has all the parts of his reproductive system at birth.

The **testicles** are located in the **scrotum**—keeping them **cooler** than body temperature, which is necessary for testicles to produce **sperm.**

OUCH!

Injury to the testicles can happen when the testicles are kicked, hit, or crushed, usually during sports, and can cause serious pain and swelling.

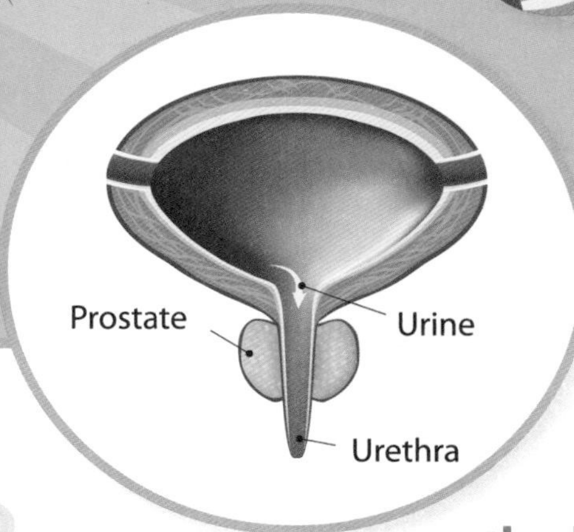

Prostate

Urine

Urethra

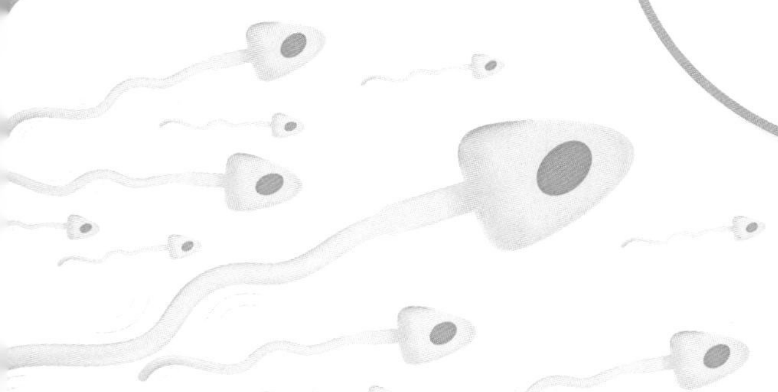

The urethra is part of two systems of the body: As part of the reproductive system, it carries semen outside the body, and as part of the urinary system, it carries urine outside the body.

Reproductive System
Female

The female reproductive system includes the vagina, the uterus, the fallopian tubes, and the ovaries.

The uterus contains some of the strongest muscles in a woman's body.

Unlike the male reproductive system, the **female reproductive system** is located only **inside** the **pelvis**.

The **cervix** connects a woman's **uterus** to her **vagina**.

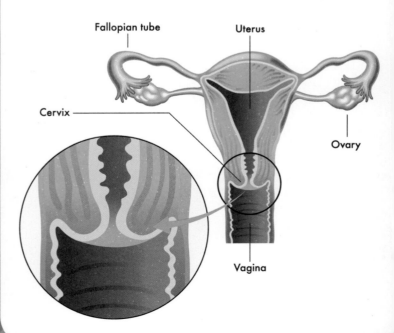

Fallopian tube

Uterus

Cervix

Ovary

Vagina

The birth canal is what a woman's vagina is called when a baby passes through it during childbirth.

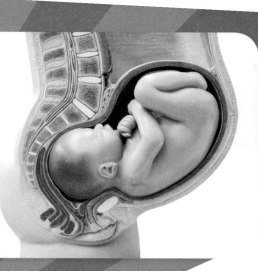

A WOMAN'S OVARIES ARE PART OF THE REPRODUCTIVE SYSTEM AND THE ENDOCRINE SYSTEM BECAUSE THEY PRODUCE THE HORMONES ESTROGEN AND PROGESTERONE.

The ovaries of a **newborn baby girl** contain **thousands** of **eggs,** but those **eggs** don't become active until **puberty.**

A girl's **menstrual cycle** begins toward the **end of puberty**—from that point on, **once a month** an **egg** is sent to the **fallopian tube** and, if unfertilized by male sperm, will dry up and pass out of the body.

Systems of the Body
Respiratory System

The respiratory system's main role is to take in oxygen and get rid of carbon dioxide. This is an important job, because the human body needs oxygen for the brain to survive.

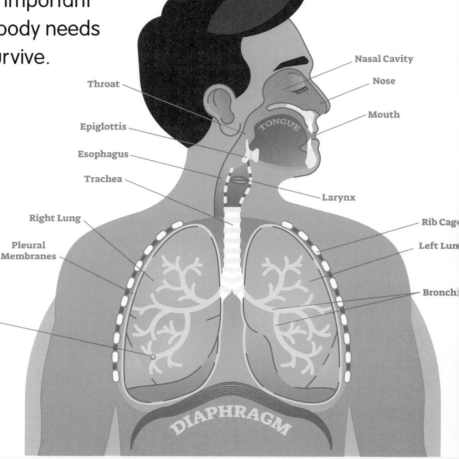

Nasal Cavity
Nose
Mouth
Throat
Epiglottis
Esophagus
Trachea
Larynx
Right Lung
Pleural Membranes
Rib Cage
Left Lung
Bronchi

TRAN-SAC-TIN BUSINESS

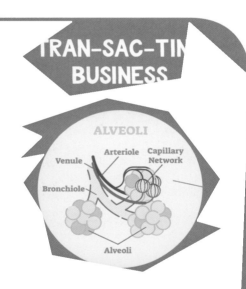

ALVEOLI
Venule
Arteriole
Capillary Network
Bronchiole
Alveoli

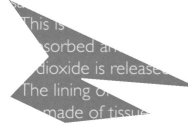

This is
sorbed a
dioxide is release
The lining of
made of tissue

CO₂-Conspirators

When you **breathe,** blood travels through **pulmonary capillaries.** The **pulmonary artery** brings blood with **carbon dioxide** in it to the **alveoli,** where the gas is removed and **exhaled** from the body. **Blood** with new, fresh **oxygen** travels to the **heart** and throughout the rest of the **body.**

Life-Lung Friends

Doctors who treat the respiratory system are called pulmonologists. They treat the entire respiratory system, not just the lungs. Pulmonologists can work in private practices, but since they are also critical in hospitals, they often work there as well.

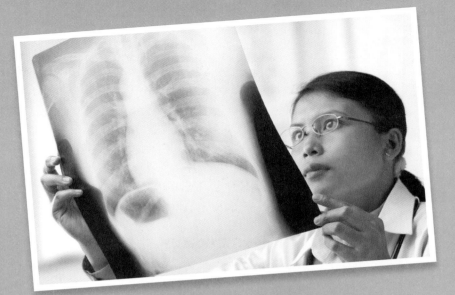

Cell Service

The tissue in your alveoli is made up of a very thin layer—only 0.2 micrometers thick—of cells called epithelial cells. Different kinds of epithelial cells can also be found as the first layers of your skin and lining all of your organs, and, depending on where they are in the body, they act as protective shields, selective filters that absorb or secrete molecules, or sensory receptors.

PLEURAL PROTECTION

The lungs are partly protected by a membrane called the pleura, or the pleural membrane. This is made up of two layers: one on the inside of the rib cage, and the other on the outside of the lungs. The layers move smoothly against each other when we breathe because of the fluid between them.

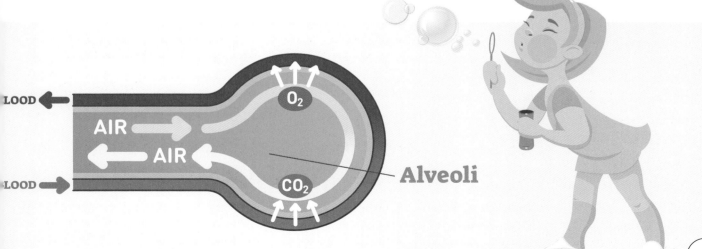

LOOD

AIR

AIR

O_2

CO_2

Alveoli

LOOD

Tummy Troubles

Heart Isn't in It

Heartburn, or gastroesophageal reflux, isn't about the heart at all—it's pain in the chest caused when acid from the stomach backs up into the esophagus. More than 60 million adults in the United States have bouts of heartburn at least once a month, and about 15 million American adults experience heartburn every day.

GROWL!

THE HOLE TRUTH

Peptic ulcers are holes that form when stomach acid and enzymes come into contact with the protective lining of the small intestine and stomach. They cause burning abdominal pain. Around 1 out of 10 Americans will suffer from a peptic or gastric ulcer in his or her life.

RUNNING ON EMPTY

Stomach "growling," also called borborygmus, is caused by wavelike contractions of the stomach and small intestine muscles—the noises are louder when your stomach is empty because the sound isn't muffled. That's why your stomach rumbles when you're hungry!

Reading the Terms

The stomach flu isn't really influenza, which is the full name of the real flu. Influenza is an illness of the respiratory system, while stomach flu is an infection of the stomach and intestine. The medical term for stomach flu is *gastroenteritis*, and it is usually caused by a viral infection. Bacteria can also cause gastroenteritis.

Bootin' the Gluten

Gluten is a protein common in grains such as wheat, barley, and rye. In people who have celiac disease, gluten causes an abnormal immune response that damages the inside of the small intestine so it can no longer absorb nutrients from food very well. However, there is no evidence that gluten is harmful to people who do not have celiac disease or gluten sensitivity.

PUT TO THE IN-TEST-INE

Crohn's disease causes parts of the digestive system to become swollen and develop ulcers. Crohn's disease is typically found in the last section of the small intestine and the first area of the large intestine, but it can develop anywhere along the digestive tract. The cause of Crohn's disease is unknown.

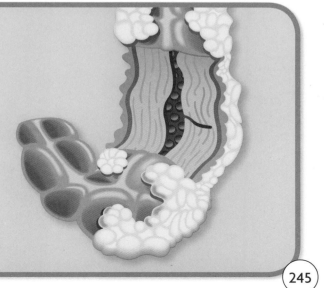

Thymus Gland

Your thymus gland is found between your lungs, behind your breastbone, which is the hard bone in the middle of your chest. It has two lobes and weighs about 1 ounce when it is fully developed.

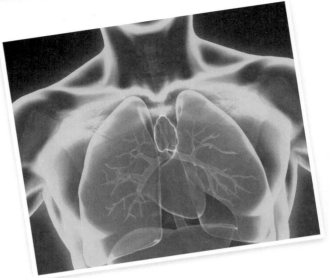

Peaked Early

The thymus is unique—it is largest in childhood and stops being functional in puberty. The thymus starts to shrink slowly starting in puberty. By the time a person is around 75, the thymus turns into fatty tissue.

FITS YOU TO A T

The thymus is responsible for producing thymosin, a hormone that helps produce T cells. Mature T cells move from the thymus to lymph nodes located throughout the body. T cells, also known as T lymphocytes, are white blood cells that fight diseases, like viruses and infections.

The thymus produces all the T cells you need by the time you reach puberty.

NOT-SO-SWEET BREAD

Some **people** actually **eat** the **thymuses** of other **animals!** Sweetbreads—which are neither sweet nor made of bread—are the organ meats of **two glands,** the **thymus** and **pancreas,** from calves, lamb, and pigs.

Capsule

Thymic corpuscle

Interlobular septum

Ligaments

Connecting the DOTS

Ligaments connect bones together. Unlike tendons, which allow muscles to move, ligaments provide stability for joints. Ligaments are also more flexible and elastic than tendons.

Ligaments

Knee joint

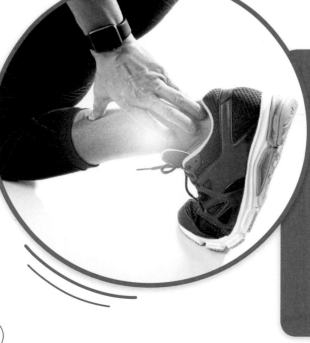

ON A ROLL

There are ligaments around your ankle, so an ankle sprain is actually a torn ankle ligament. If your foot rolls under your ankle while you're playing a sport—especially a sport that involves jumping—you may sprain your ankle and injure one of these ankle ligaments.

Strike Out

Baseball players, especially pitchers, often injure the ligaments of their shoulders. When these ligaments are stretched too far, they become unstable. These ligaments connect the arm bone to the shoulder blade and hold the collarbone to the top of the shoulder.

Throw Down

Baseball players can damage their elbow ligaments from repetitive throwing. The elbow has two main ligaments: the ulnar collateral ligament (UCL) and the lateral collateral ligament (LCL), both of which can be torn if used too much.

REST UP

If you sprain or strain a ligament, you should avoid putting weight on the injured area. Apply ice and wrap the injured area to slow down inflammation, and raise it above heart level to lessen the swelling.

Fill in the Blanks

Ligaments

**Fill in the missing letters to complete the facts below.
For help, look at the previous pages about ligaments.**

Ligaments provide stability for __ __O__ __ __ __T__ __.

A sprained __ __ __K__ __ __E__ is actually a torn ligament,

and it commonly occurs in sports that include jumping.

Elbow ligaments can be damaged by repeated motions in this sport:
__B__ __ __ __E__ __ __A__ __ __.

There are two kinds of ligaments in the elbow: the __ __ __L__ __ __A__ __

and __ __ __T__ __ __ __ __L__ collateral ligaments.

Ligaments in this part of the body connect to the arm and

to the collarbone: __ __ __ __U__ __ __ __R__.

If you sprain a ligament, you should avoid putting

__ __E__ __ __G__ __ __ on that area.

Ligaments connect __ __ __N__ __ __ in your body.

Bones are tough! They bend under pressure, but if the pressure is too much or too sudden, your bones can snap. This type of break is called a fracture, and it can happen by doing everyday things, like riding a bike or swinging across monkey bars.

Cast On

If you suspect you have a broken bone, you should seek medical attention. A doctor will do an X-ray to see what is broken and how complicated the fracture is. The doctor will set the bone and then put on a cast to keep the bone still for however long it needs to heal. If you break a larger bone or your bone is broken in multiple places, you may need to have metal pins put in to help set the bone. This is usually done through surgery.

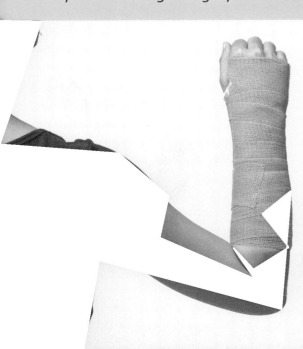

DID YOU KNOW?

Casts can be made of plaster, fiberglass, or plastic, which are all hard substances designed to protect the break and allow it time to repair.

Why We Bruise

Bruise Like a Peach

Some people, especially those with pale skin, seem to bruise more easily than others. It could be that some people have weaker blood vessels than others. Occasionally, a person can have a condition that causes her or him to have trouble clotting and to bruise more often.

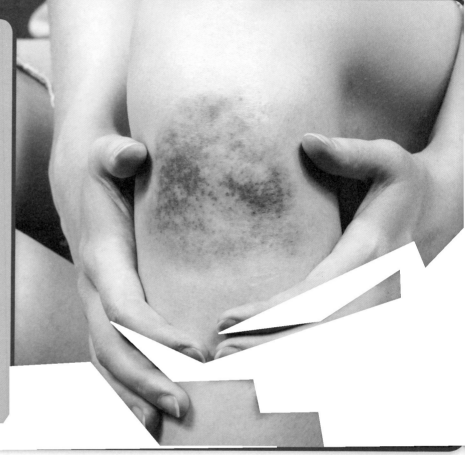

K-ey Vitamins

Other factors can affect how easily you bruise: Certain medications, like aspirin, are known to thin blood, which can make you more likely to bruise. Not having enough vitamin K can also cause you to bruise more easily, since your blood needs vitamin K in order to properly clot.

Not So Thick-Skinned

Aging skin is more prone to bruising. As blood vessels get older and weaker, they become more fragile. When the skin ages and collagen in the skin breaks down, the skin becomes thinner, so bruises are more easily seen.

Have the Bruise Blues

When the small blood vessels close to the surface of your skin, called capillaries, are traumatized, you get a bruise. Blood can leak out of those damaged vessels into the area around them, and that's what causes your skin to color black, blue, purple, and even yellow when you bruise. The yellow color happens when the body sends white blood cells to take apart the red blood cells.

Most doctors agree that if you bruise easily or often, it is typically nothing to worry about.

Cruising for a Bruising

If you do intense, or tough, exercise, you may be more prone to bruising. Athletes and weight lifters, for example, can put stress on their blood vessels, causing microscopic tears in the vessels that result in bruises.

DID YOU KNOW?

Bruises heal with time. You can ice an area as soon as you injure it to try to minimize bruising, but besides that, there isn't much that can be done except to wait!

FUN FACTS about Yoga

...istic fo...
...th...
...thing
...and meditation.

Some people believe that yoga keeps POSITIVE ENERGY flowing through the eight CHAKRAS, or energy centers, of your body.

Yoga may cut your risk of heart disease by improving your cardiovascular health.

Breathing is very important in yoga. Ancient yoga practitioners thought that the body had a finite number of breaths, so it made sense to take long, deep, slow breaths to stretch out the number of breaths a person had.

SOME PEOPLE TAKE THEIR DOWNWARD DOG—A COMMON RESTING POSE IN YOGA—LITERALLY. THERE IS SUCH A THING AS DOGA, WHERE PEOPLE PRACTICE YOGA WITH THEIR PET DOGS!

One study found that after eight weeks of a daily yoga practice, people with insomnia, or extreme trouble sleeping, had improved sleep quality.

SOME STUDIES SUGGEST THAT YOGA HELPS YOUR IMMUNE SYSTEM.

Hindu mythology calls Lord Shiva the Adi Guru, otherwise known as the first yoga teacher.

There are many different styles of yoga, but some of the most popular include Hatha, Ashtanga, Bikram, Iyengar, and Kundalini.

Injuries and How Your Body Heals

Not So Cute

Sudden injuries, like strains or sprains, are called acute injuries. If you suffer the same kind of injury many times, or for a long period of time, you have a chronic injury.

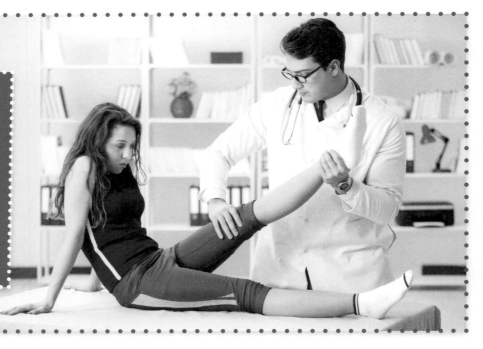

Special Tissue

If skin is severely damaged, it heals by forming scar tissue. Scar tissue is not the same as normal skin tissue—it doesn't have sweat glands or hair.

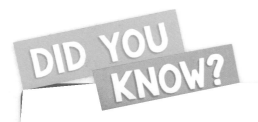

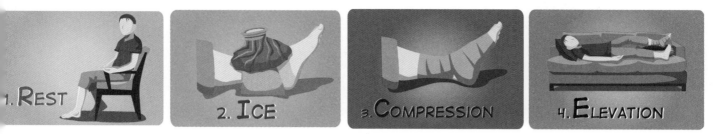

1. REST   2. ICE   3. COMPRESSION   4. ELEVATION

R-I-C-E is Nice

ports injuries are very common, and one-fourth of them involve the hand and wrist. The first step to treating injuries is to use the R-I-C-E method: rest, ice, compression (wrapping the injury), and elevation (raising the injury above the level of the heart).

Be a Good Sport: Don't Get Injured

In 2012, football, basketball, soccer, and baseball caused the most emergency room visits in athletes 19 and younger. Most of these injuries involved the ankle, knee, finger, head, and face. The most common injuries doctors diagnose in kids are strains and sprains, followed by broken bones, scrapes, bruises, and concussions.

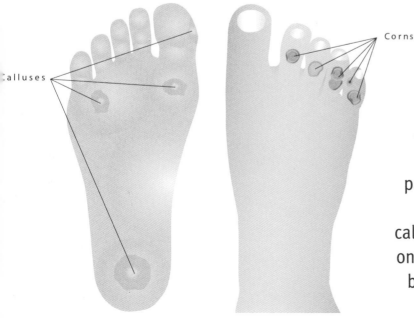

Corns

Calluses

Thick Skin

Areas of the skin that experience repeated pressure such as friction, or something rubbing against them, can form tough, thick skin known as a callus. A corn is a small, circular patch of thick skin with a hard center, usually found on the foot. Like a callus, it forms from repeated pressure on the skin. It earned the name "corn" because it looks like a kernel of corn!

257

A Heavy Topic
Strength Training

GOING STRONG

Weight or resistance training—also known as weight lifting or strength training—improves the fitness of muscles by performing exercises that target a specific muscle or muscle group. These exercises are typically performed against resistance, which can be in the form of a machine or a person's own body weight.

Pull Your Weight

As people age, they lose lean muscle mass, which is known as sarcopenia. Regular weight training can help prevent the loss of lean muscle mass due to aging. According to the Centers for Disease Control and Prevention (CDC), people should do activities that strengthen muscles at least two days per week, focusing on as many areas of the body as possible—such as the legs, arms, shoulders, back, hips, and core.

FEELING THE BURN

While you are strength training, you burn calories, which boosts your metabolism. Even after you stop lifting weights, your body continues to burn calories.

Word Search

Physical Activity

Look at the puzzle below and see if you can find these words all about physical activity. Circle the words going across, up and down, and diagonally. Some words may be backwards!

EXERTION   PEDOMETER   STRENGTH

METABOLISM   PILATES   TRAINING

MUSCLES   RECOVERY   ULTRAMARATHON

OLYMPICS   RESISTANCE   WALKING

OXYGEN   RUNNING   WEIGHTS

```
C N V T V S R N A Q H V N D Y
P Q S F R U T C M C A O N R P
M I R E N A E H C L H B E Y E
E H L N L U I R G T K V G S D
Z O I A V C E N A I O L Y Q O
M N I Z T N S R I C E T X V M
G E D I I E A U E N M W O H E
W W T N W M S R M R G K U S T
D H U A A R E S I S T A N C E
H M D R B S T R E N G T H I R
N G T I J O G N I K L A W P Y
V L B A P H L Z R R I H U M L
U U S H C R Q I X C G P G Y P
N V R G Z E R J S O F O W L T
N O I T R E X E S M D D D O F
```

ACL

stands for anterior cruciate ligament, the ligament most commonly hurt in knee injuries.

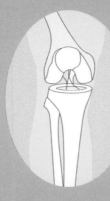

ADHD

is the abbreviation for attention deficit hyperactivity disorder, a disorder with symptoms such as difficulty paying attention and staying still.

BP

stands for blood pressure, one of the vital signs.

CBC

stands for complete blood count.

HA

is a shorter way of saying headache.

CPAP

stands for continuous positive airway pressure, which is a treatment for sleep apnea, a condition where breathing is interrupted while sleeping.

ICU

stands for intensive care unit, a critical area of a hospital reserved for very ill patients.

LBP

stands for low back pain, which is a common medical condition.

P

stands for pulse, one of the vital signs.

PT

is the abbreviation for physical therapy.

PFT

stands for pulmonary function test, which can tell how the lungs are performing.

T

stands for temperature, one of the vital signs.

Scoliosis

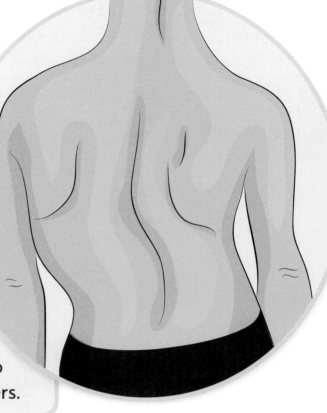

Backbend

Scoliosis is a curvature of the spine. In people who have scoliosis, the spine curves sideways. The curve can be small (less than 20 degrees), medium (between 20 and 50 degrees), or large (greater than 50 degrees). Sometimes this curve can cause changes to the person's back and also to the pelvis, waist, rib cage, and shoulders.

Types of Scoliosis

There are several kinds of scoliosis, depending on which part of the spine is curved. A curve in the top of the spine is called thoracic scoliosis, while one at the base of the spine is called lumbar scoliosis. Thoracolumbar scoliosis is in between, and combined scoliosis involves multiple different curves.

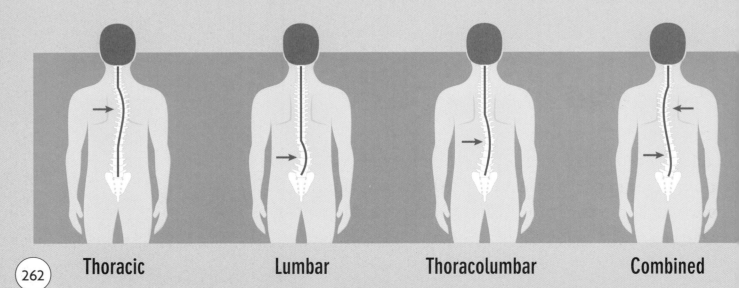

Thoracic   Lumbar   Thoracolumbar   Combined

Idiopathic Scoliosis

Sometimes, doctors can't find the cause of scoliosis. This is called idiopathic scoliosis, and it usually runs in the family. If one of your relatives has idiopathic scoliosis, you have a 1-in-10 chance of having it, while people without a family history have a 1-in-1,000 chance.

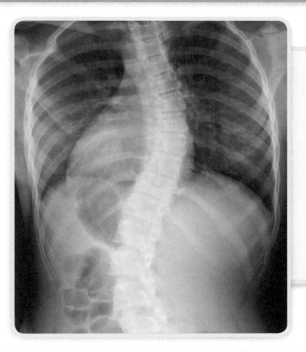

Congenital Scoliosis

People with congenital scoliosis are born with differently shaped bones, though the curved spine may not appear until later in childhood or adolescence. The irregular bones can be recognized by looking at X-rays.

Neuromuscular Scoliosis

If X-rays show regularly shaped bones, the scoliosis may be caused by a muscle condition, like muscular dystrophy or cerebral palsy, which is usually genetic and diagnosed early.

Ahead of the Curve

Sometimes, the spine will curve more as a person ages. Some curves require treatment, while others do not. If the curve is less than 20 degrees, doctors will watch the curve to see if it progresses. Medium curves might require a brace, and curves greater than 50 degrees might need surgery.

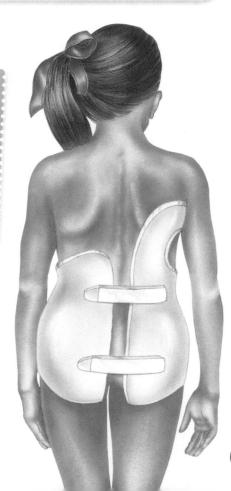

Chiropractic Medicine

Back to Basics

Chiropractic medicine treats the musculoskeletal and nervous systems. It focuses on how disorders of these systems impact a person's health. The symptoms of these disorders can include back pain, neck pain, joint pain, and headaches.

Did You Hear About This?

Daniel David "DD" Palmer did the first chiropractic adjustment in September 1895. He treated a janitor who had become deaf after suffering a back injury 17 years earlier. Palmer adjusted what he thought were vertebrae that were out of place in the janitor's back. The janitor claimed his hearing improved. In 1897, Palmer started the first chiropractic college, located in Iowa, called the Palmer College of Chiropractic.

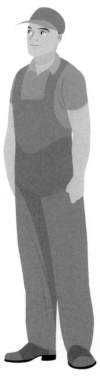

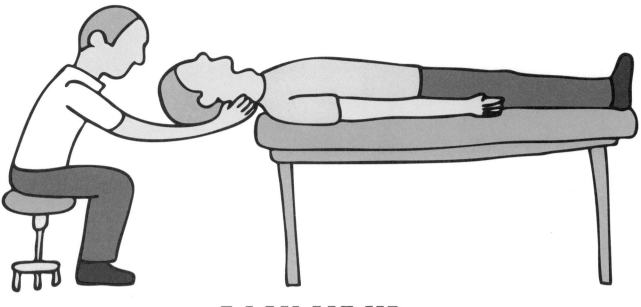

BACK ME UP

People often go to the chiropractor for an adjustment. "Adjustment" is another name for spinal manipulation, or treatment by moving the spine. When a chiropractor adjusts you, he or she is working to improve or restore mobility to your joints. Your joints may either be hypermobile, meaning they move too much, or their movement may be restricted, not able to move enough.

Hands-on Experience

"Chiropractic" is the combination of two Greek words: *cheir,* which means "hand," and *praxis,* which means "practice." DD Palmer, the developer of chiropractic medicine, selected the name. While some form of hands-on manipulation had been done on humans for years, no one had ever made it a scientific discipline.

There are about 77,000 doctors of chiropractic medicine in the United States as of 2018. In any given year, chiropractors provide treatment to more than 35 million American adults and children.

Chiro-practice Makes Perfect

Doctors of chiropractic medicine are called DCs, but most people call them chiropractors. Chiropractors attend a four-year graduate school program and, like MDs, have to pass exams before they are licensed to practice. In addition to providing hands-on care for a patient's condition, they can give advice on a patient's nutrition, diet, and lifestyle.

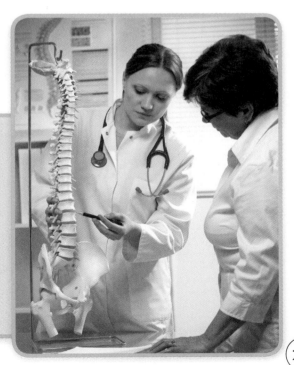

Going to the Dentist

A Team for Your Teeth

Your teeth have their own doctor! Dentists are doctors who take care of teeth. Pediatric dentists take care of children's teeth. A dental hygienist works with the dentist to clean your teeth before the doctor does his or her examination of your teeth. Dental checkups should be done every six months for children and adults.

Pl-ack!

Teeth cleaning and polishing is done to remove plaque from your teeth. Plaque contains bacteria, so if it is left on your teeth, it can cause tooth decay, known as a cavity. Plaque is thin and sticky and coats your teeth; the dental hygienist removes it with a tooth scraper.

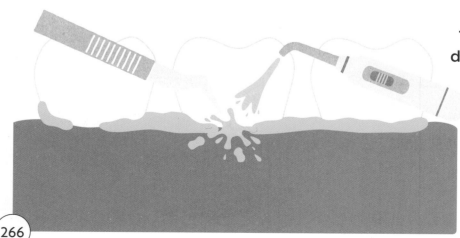

With a Fine-Tooth Comb

The dental hygienist polishes the teeth in addition to cleaning them. He or she will use tools like a tooth scraper, a special toothbrush, and a mirror to see all surfaces of the teeth.

Treat Yourself

Dental exams often include a fluoride treatment. Fluoride is a mineral that is good for your teeth—it helps keep your teeth strong and cavity-free. A fluoride solution, usually a gel or foam, is put on your teeth and left there for a few minutes so this natural mineral can penetrate your teeth.

FILL 'ER UP

Cavities are rotted parts of your teeth. When you have a cavity, the dentist removes the decayed part of your tooth using special tools. Then, the hole is filled with materials like plastic resin, porcelain, gold, or silver.

Picture This

Sometimes, you will have X-rays taken at your dental appointment. These pictures of your teeth can show the dentist signs of tooth decay and gum disease.

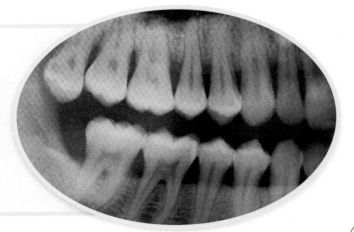

The History of Dentistry

Straight from the Donkey's Mouth

People think George Washington's dentures were made of wood, but that's a myth. Washington had four pairs of custom-made dentures made from gold, lead, ivory, and a combination of teeth from humans, donkeys, and hippopotamuses.

Sink Your Teeth Into It

Ancient Egyptians understood that it was important to brush their teeth, but they didn't have toothbrushes or toothpaste like we do. Instead, they made their own mixtures! They would first mix eggshells and the hooves of oxen to make a powder. Then, they mixed the powder with liquid to get a gritty paste and used this to remove leftover food from their teeth.

Brush with Fame

William Addis, an Englishman, is credited with developing the first modern toothbrush. He used a bone handle and attached boars' bristles. His toothbrush was mass-produced, but it wasn't until the 1930s that toothbrushes had nylon bristles and user-friendly handles.

Dental Hygiene

Look at the puzzle below and see if you can find these words all about dental hygiene. Circle the words going across, up and down, and diagonally. Some words may be backwards!

BACTERIA   DENTURES   MOUTHWASH

BRISTLES   FILLING   PLAQUE

CAVITY   FLOSS   TEETH

DECAY   FLUORIDE   TOOTHBRUSH

DENTIST   HYGIENIST   TOOTHPASTE

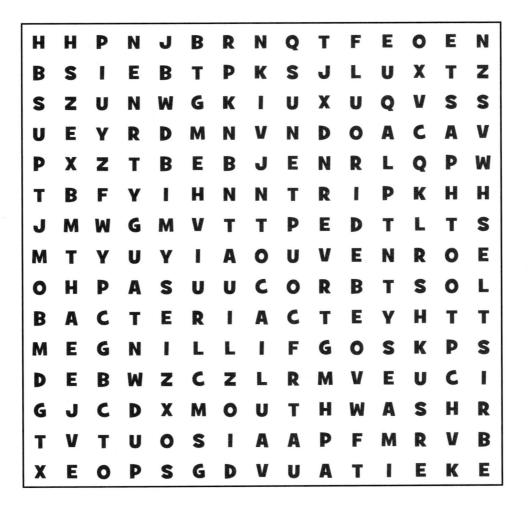

```
H H P N J B R N Q T F E O E N
B S I E B T P K S J L U X T Z
S Z U N W G K I U X U Q V S S
U E Y R D M N V N D O A C A V
P X Z T B E B J E N R L Q P W
T B F Y I H N N T R I P K H H
J M W G M V T T P E D T L T S
M T Y U Y I A O U V E N R O E
O H P A S U U C O R B T S O L
B A C T E R I A C T E Y H T T
M E G N I L L I F G O S K P S
D E B W Z C Z L R M V E U C I
G J C D X M O U T H W A S H R
T V T U O S I A A P F M R V B
X E O P S G D V U A T I E K E
```

At the Core of Exercise
Pilates

CONTROLLED EXERCISE

Pilates is a series of exercises that improves flexibility, strength, and endurance. Pilates focuses on posture alignment, core muscles (the abdominals, back, and pelvic muscles), and balance. Joseph Pilates created it in the 1920s and originally called this type of exercise contrology, meaning "the study of control." The exercise was later renamed after the man who invented it.

Movement Medicine

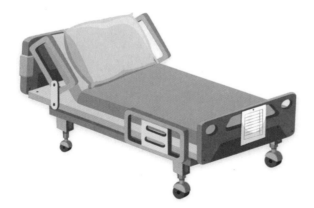

The first Pilates machines were actually hospital beds. Joseph Pilates reconfigured the springs of these beds to allow patients who were bedridden due to World War I injuries to exercise to improve their health and recover from their injuries faster.

The Great Mix-up

While typically lumped together as mind-body exercises, Pilates and yoga are not the same. Pilates is not a version of yoga, though some principals are the same. Pilates is considered a physical fitness system that develops core strength, while yoga is a meditative practice that uses movement.

It's Magic

The first piece of Pilates equipment Joseph Pilates ever made was called the magic circle. He took steel bands from the outsides of beer kegs and used them to enhance his exercise program.

A Method to His Mat-ness

Pilates exercises performed on a mat are common. In fact, the 34 mat-based exercises in Joseph Pilates's original exercise method are still done today. However, Joseph Pilates also developed exercises for a special machine he created that he called a reformer.

CORE ISSUE

Joseph Pilates thought his exercise method should focus on control of the mind and body. He developed exercises that specifically targeted a person's core, which includes the stomach muscles and lower back. He focused on spinal alignment and proper breathing techniques.

The Highs and Lows of Cholesterol

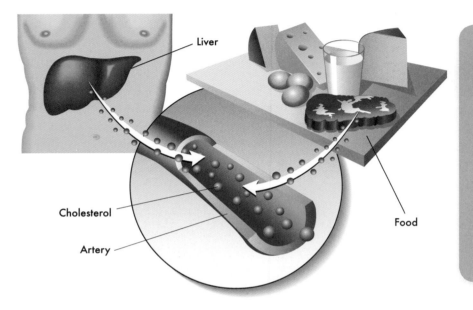

Liver

Cholesterol

Artery

Food

BUILDING BLOCK

Cholesterol often gets a bad reputation, but your body actually needs cholesterol to build cells. Your liver makes some of this waxy substance, but the rest you get from food, such as meat, poultry, and full-fat dairy products.

It's a Lifestyle Choice

Generally, a person's lifestyle choices—what they eat, if they exercise, and if they have unhealthy habits like smoking—dictate their cholesterol levels. In some cases, cholesterol levels are genetic. Familial hypercholesterolemia (FH) is inherited from the genes of a mother, father, or grandparent, and can cause high cholesterol.

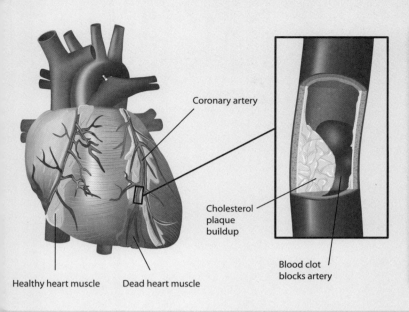

Coronary artery

Cholesterol plaque buildup

Blood clot blocks artery

Healthy heart muscle   Dead heart muscle

The Good, the Bad, and the Body

Cholesterol is considered either "good" or "bad." Bad cholesterol is called LDL cholesterol. HDL is considered good cholesterol. If you have too much bad cholesterol and not enough good cholesterol, the bad cholesterol will line the inside of the heart and block arteries, which can cause major health problems.

Time for a Change

High cholesterol can be treated with medication, but often doctors will prescribe lifestyle changes for a patient who has high cholesterol. These changes can include: eating a heart-healthy diet focused on fruits, vegetables, whole grains, and lean proteins; quitting smoking; getting more physical activity; and losing excess weight.

DID YOU KNOW?

A fun way to remember which cholesterol is which is to remember that HDL (good cholesterol) starts with "H," which is the first letter in "healthy"!

Risky Business

Having high cholesterol puts you at a higher risk for heart disease, heart attack, and stroke. For people with high cholesterol, smoking makes that risk even greater. For most people, however, cholesterol level is controllable with lifestyle changes.

Run for Your Life!

In the Running

While studies show that both men and women run their fastest when they are in their 20s, people can run well into old age. The oldest person on record to run a marathon is Fauja Singh, who completed one in under eight hours at age 101.

RUNNING IN PLACE

Running on a treadmill is different than running outside. When you run on a treadmill, there is no wind resistance because the machine pulls the belt under your feet. Treadmills can be lower impact than running outside because they are padded, but they certainly don't have the same scenery as running outdoors!

Run Out of Town

Most people think the marathon was an ancient Olympic sport, but it wasn't around back then. The long-distance race known as the marathon was not introduced until the 1896 Olympic Games in Athens, Greece. The race was run between the Greek cities of Marathon and Athens, the same 26.2 miles that an ancient Greek soldier, Pheidippides, ran to share the news of a Greek victory over the Persians in 490 BC. The length of a marathon was made standard during the 1908 Olympic games, which were held in London.

Run, Crackle, Pop

Crepitus is a condition common with runners. Crepitus causes the knees of runners to crack when they bend. This happens because the cartilage between the thighbone and the knee bone ages and, as it does, it causes these two bones to grind into each other, creating the popping sound.

RUN LIKE AN EGYPTIAN

It is thought that running races took place in ancient Egypt—there is evidence that races of more than 3,000 meters took place in 3800 BC. Today, runners participate in races of different lengths. Some of the most popular races include marathons, half marathons, ultramarathons, triathlons, duathlons, 10-kilometer races, and 5-kilometer races.

Spot the Difference
Marathon

Find and circle 10 differences between these two pictures of people running a marathon.

Answers on page 317

FUN FACTS about Walking

According to studies, walking regularly helps older women maintain their memories and avoid declining mental function.

WALKING CAN HELP YOU IMPROVE THINKING BY INCREASING BLOOD FLOW TO THE BRAIN.

Walking helps prevent bone loss and associated diseases, like osteoporosis, because it promotes bone formation.

A study conducted by Harvard University demonstrated that women can cut their risk of heart disease by 40% by walking moderately for about 30 minutes per day.

New technology, like digital pedometers that track a person's daily steps, makes it easy to track how many steps you walk a day. Experts say that taking 10,000 steps a day will improve your health.

One study showed that women who walked an average of

10,000 steps

a day had

40% less

body fat than women who walked fewer than 6,000 steps.

Under Pressure

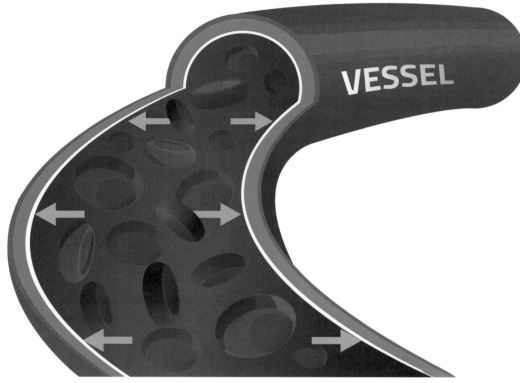

VESSEL

A High-Pressure Job

Blood exerts force inside your blood vessels—this is your blood pressure. If your blood pressure is too high, there's too much pressure inside your blood vessels, and this makes it more likely for you to have certain diseases.

Take This to Heart

If you are generally healthy, low blood pressure is a good thing. There are a few cases, however, when low blood pressure means there is a problem.

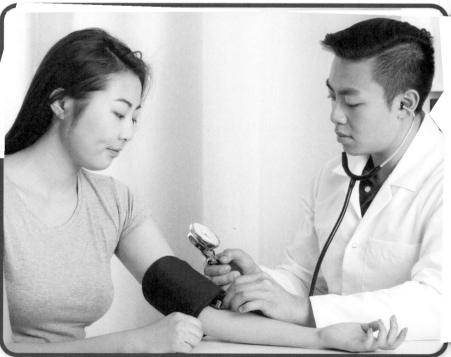

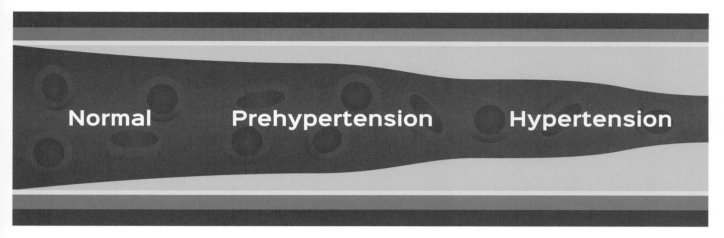

Normal   Prehypertension   Hypertension

YOUR PEERS' PRESSURES

Almost half of all Americans have high blood pressure, also called hypertension. While some people have symptoms, most of the time there is nothing obvious that would indicate someone has hypertension. A doctor should officially diagnose hypertension.

Change It Up

In most cases, you can't cure high blood pressure. A doctor can prescribe medicine, however, and there are many lifestyle changes a person can make to help limit the damage caused by high blood pressure. These lifestyle changes include eating a healthy diet, being physically active, managing stress, and staying at a healthy weight.

On the Cuff Remarks

The cuff used by medical professionals to measure your blood pressure is called a sphygmomanometer. It was developed in the early 20th century. There are two numbers in a blood pressure reading: systolic (top number) measures the pressure inside your arteries, and diastolic (bottom number) measures the pressure between heartbeats.

Mind Over Matter

A Great Re-mind-er

People have meditated for thousands of years. Meditation originally was developed to help people contemplate the world around them and the forces of nature they may not have understood. Today, people use meditation to relax and de-stress.

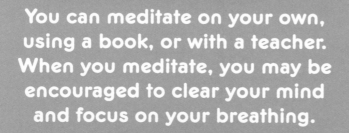

You can meditate on your own, using a book, or with a teacher. When you meditate, you may be encouraged to clear your mind and focus on your breathing.

Don't Mind if I Do

Meditation is considered a complementary medicine focusing on mind-body wellness. A 2011 study found that after eight weeks of doing regular mindfulness meditation, the parts of the brain responsible for learning, memory, and regulating emotions improved, while stress and anxiety decreased.

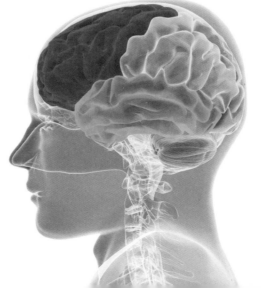

MOVING MEDITATION

Sometimes, meditation involves movement. Qigong and tai chi both combine meditation and physical movement to calm the mind and body. As you may remember, yoga is another form of meditative practice that involves movement.

Body Benefits

While meditation has many emotional and stress relieving benefits, it can also help manage some medical conditions, like high blood pressure and tension headaches. Studies have shown that the brains of people who meditate maintain their brain matter volume better than non-meditators as they age.

Mind Your Business

There are many different kinds of meditation. In guided meditation, for example, a teacher or guide will encourage you to create mental images, like daydreams, of people, places, or activities that relax you. Mindfulness meditation is based on the concepts of awareness and acceptance: In mindfulness meditation, you are asked to simply observe your thoughts as they enter your mind, but not to react to them.

Sports Injuries
Concussions

No Need to Go Head to Head

When people think of concussions, they likely think of collision sports, like football or hockey. However, concussions can happen regardless of sport or competition level. In fact, current studies show that anywhere from 1.6 million to nearly 4 million recreational concussions, including those related to sports, happen each year—and that number is increasing.

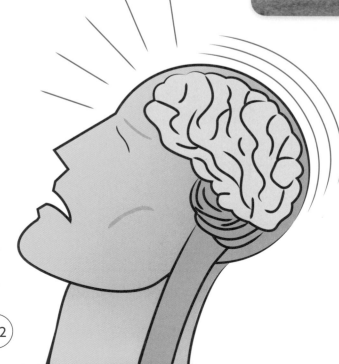

ALL IN YOUR HEAD

The brain is soft, and it's surrounded by the skull and spinal fluid for protection. If you hit your head hard enough, your brain can be jostled around inside your skull, causing bruising, nerve injury, and damage to the nearby blood vessels. When this happens, your brain doesn't function normally, and you can experience concussion symptoms, such as changes in balance, vision, and consciousness.

Concussions are graded on three levels:

GRADE 1

Concussion lasts less than 15 minutes and doesn't cause you to lose consciousness.

GRADE 2

Your symptoms last longer, but there is still no loss of consciousness.

GRADE 3

You lose consciousness.

DON'T RUSH A-HEAD

It is important to let your body heal after a concussion. Concussions are cumulative, meaning once you've had a concussion, you have a greater risk of suffering another one in the future. Do not begin your normal activities again until you have fully recovered from a concussion.

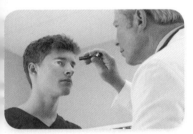

The Other Kind of Football

According to recent research into high school athletics, the sport with the highest rate of concussions is not football, which ranks second. It is actually girls' soccer!

Concussion Discussion

If you suffer a bump to your head that causes a disruption in your normal brain activity, you may have a concussion, the most common type of traumatic brain injury (TBI). TBIs can be mild, causing a short period of memory loss or consciousness, to severe.

Football-ing the Bill

In 2016, the National Football League (NFL) reported 244 concussions in both practices and games. That same year, the commissioner of the NFL announced a plan to help make football safer for players by trying to prevent concussions. The NFL and its teams promised to donate $100 million to medical research focused on neuroscience and advancements in engineering that might make the game safer.

FUN FACTS about
World Record Bodies

The longest nose was measured on a man—3.46 inches long from the bridge, or top, of the nose to the tip.

The record holder for the longest tongue has a tongue that is almost 4 inches long!

A man in India holds the record for the most teeth: He has 37 teeth, which is five more than most people have!

The longest beard was measured on a man in Canada—his beard, when measured for the record, was 7 feet, 9 inches long.

The world's longest legs belong to a Russian model who is 6 feet, 8 inches tall!

The tallest man on record is a Turkish man who measures over 8 feet tall.

The record holder for the heaviest man is from Mexico and weighs 1,311 pounds!

In India, the shortest woman alive measured 24.7 inches, or just a little over 2 feet tall, on her 18th birthday.

The record holder for largest feet is a teenager who has to have his shoes made just for him. Each foot measures nearly 40 centimeters (almost 1½ feet)!

A woman in China, who began growing her hair out when she was 13, holds the record for the longest hair—more than 18 feet long.

Hormones

Hair-mones

Men and women have different hormones, affecting everything from how they look to how they act. For example, a type of hormone called an androgen causes hair growth. Men have more androgen hormones, so they grow more hair on their faces and bodies than women.

Set in Bone

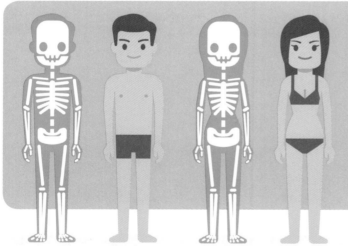

Hormones affect bone development differently in men and women. Testosterone is the primary hormone that controls the shape of a man's bones, while estrogen controls the shape of a woman's bones. High levels of estrogen cause women's bones to harden earlier than men's. A woman's bones are set by the time she is 18, while men's bones grow until they are 21.

JUST POINTING THIS OUT

Studies have shown that if your right pointer finger is shorter than your right ring finger, you were exposed to more testosterone before birth.

Hormones

Fill in the missing letters to complete the facts below.
For help, look at the pages about hormones and puberty.

__ O __ M __ N __ __ are different in men and
women and affect everything from how much hair they have on
their bodies to how their bones are shaped.

A __ __ R __ G __ __ __ are
the type of hormone responsible for hair growth.

High levels of __ S __ __ O __ E __ cause a
woman's bones to harden before a man's bones harden.

A woman's bones are set by the time she is __ __ years old, but

a man's bones aren't set until he is __ __ years old.

The shorter your right pointer finger is relative to your right ring finger,

the more __ __ S T __ __ __ __ E __ __ N __ you
were exposed to before birth.

In both boys and girls, the __ __ I __ U __ __ __ __ Y
gland produces hormones when puberty begins.

The hormones that cause puberty also cause __ __ N __, or
pimples, to appear because of increased oil production during puberty.

Incredible Bodies Olympic Athletes

You're Only Young Once

The most common age for a Summer Olympic Games medalist is 23, and the most common age for a medalist at the Winter Olympic Games is 24. However, the average age of a medalist varies greatly from sport to sport: A typical female medal winner in gymnastics is 20, while the average age for a male or female medalist in equestrian, or horseback, competitions is in the mid-30s.

A Man for All Seasons

Rarely do athletes compete in both the Summer and Winter Olympic Games, but 136 athletes have. Eddie Eagan is the only athlete to have won a gold medal in both a summer and a winter sport. He won a gold medal in boxing in the 1920 Summer Games and later won gold in the bobsleigh competition in the 1932 Winter Games.

DID YOU KNOW?

If you want to win an Olympic medal, maybe you should change your name to John! Athletes named John have won a total of 272 medals. Robert, Vladimir, Olga, Elena, and Maria are other names that happen to be common among winning Olympic athletes.

ONLY THE BEST

Only 137,000 people have participated in the modern Olympic Games. Most people, around 100,000 of the total participants, have competed in one game only. However, a Canadian athlete named Ian Miller holds the record for participating in the most Olympic Games—he appeared in 10 of them!

Full Potential

Olympic athletes need a lot of fuel: During the 2016 Rio Olympic Games, the Olympic Village, where the athletes stayed, served 60,000 meals per day! However, each athlete consumes a different amount of calories, depending on the specific requirements of his or her sport. For example, a gymnast might eat 2,500 calories each day, while an athlete participating in an endurance sport, like cycling, might eat up to 8,000 calories per day.

Great Scott!

Thomas Scott was the oldest person ever to compete in his or her first Olympic Games. An American who competed in archery, Scott participated in his first Olympics in 1904 at age 71!

The Eyes Have It

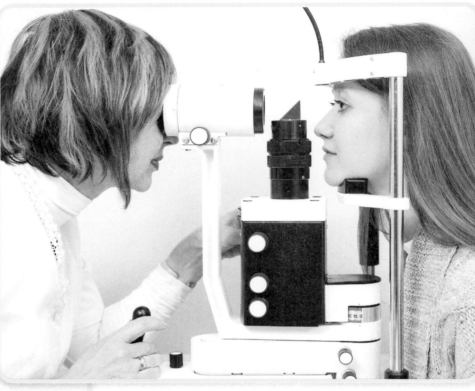

The Doctor Will See You

Optometrists, also known as Doctors of Optometry (ODs), are health care professionals who treat the eyes. Optometrists can prescribe glasses and contact lenses, and they can treat eye diseases like glaucoma and perform minor surgeries.

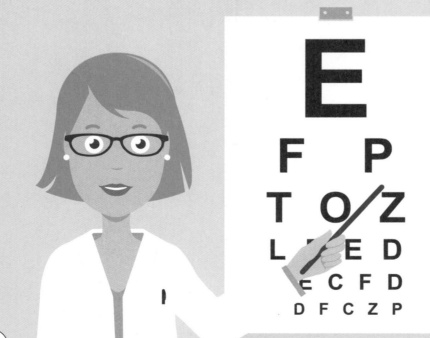

YOU'VE GOT "OPHTH"IONS

Ophthalmologists are physicians. They perform more complicated eye surgeries but also diagnose and treat diseases of the eye and fit glasses or contact lenses.

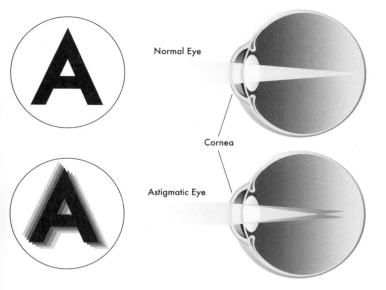

Inescapable Stigma

Almost everyone is born with some version of astigmatism. This means the eyeball isn't shaped like a perfectly round ball. This imperfect shape bends light more in one way than another, causing only part of any object to be in focus and making faraway objects look blurry or wavy. Glasses, contact lenses, or surgery can easily fix astigmatism.

Color Me Surprised!

Sometimes, a person can have irises that are two different colors. This is called heterochromia, and it can be total, where the entire iris of one eye is a different color than the other, or it can be partial, where only part of the iris is a different color. If only the inner ring of the iris is a different color, it is called central heterochromia. You can be born with heterochromia or develop it later in life, usually due to an injury or disease. Unless the heterochromia is caused by a condition that needs treatment, it can go untreated and won't affect a person's health.

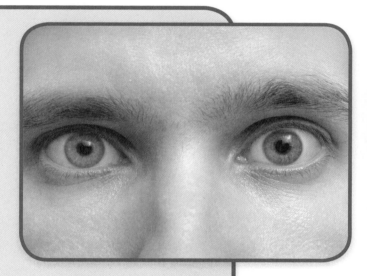

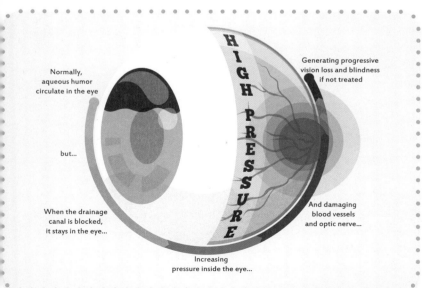

THAT HIT a Nerve

When the optic nerve of the eye is damaged, it can cause loss of vision, sometimes to the point of blindness, because you need the optic nerve to be healthy in order to see properly. The group of diseases that can cause this to happen is called glaucoma.

Hips

HIP LINGO

The hip bone is called the pelvic bone. The hip bone is made up of three parts: the ilium, which is the side of the hip bone you can feel; the ischium, which is the bone you sit on; and the pubis, which is in the middle of the hip bone, and sits below the tailbone.

Having a Ball

The hip joint is the body's biggest ball-and-socket joint—and that's a good thing. It means the joint can move easily. You use your hip joints for all kinds of movement, including walking, so the hip joints need to be able to handle repeating the same motions over and over again.

Hip Hops

The hip joint is designed to handle friction. When the hip bone moves in the socket, the cartilage of the hip joint acts like a shock absorber. As you age, you can break down the cartilage and overuse the tendons and muscles. These are typical causes of hip pain, which is very common.

Pair Matching

Skeletons

There are 3 sets of skeletons below. Draw a line to connect the skeleton on the left with its identical twin on the right.

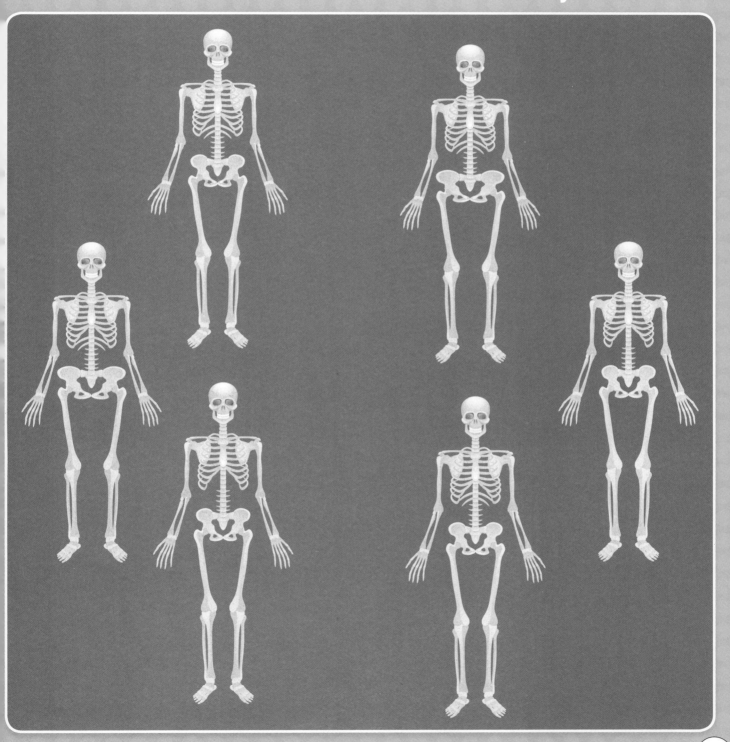

FUN FACTS about Eating Organic

Organic food has been shown to have slightly higher levels of some nutrients than conventionally grown food, especially flavonoids, which are considered antioxidants. Antioxidants help to prevent reactions to oxygen or harmful chemicals in the air.

Organic food is better for the planet, especially when it is locally sourced and seasonal. Locally sourced food does not have to travel far to reach your plate, saving fuel emissions. If it is seasonal, it is planted and harvested when the weather and climate are most appropriate, instead of relying on energy-intensive ways of mimicking other climates to produce out-of-season foods.

Pregnant women and very young people can benefit the most from eating organic food. Studies have shown that even small amounts of pesticides, or chemicals used to kill off insects, like those found on conventionally grown produce, can harm young children and fetuses, or unborn babies.

Organic grains have been shown to have less cadmium, which is a toxic substance found naturally in soil, than conventionally grown grains.

Organic or not, it's important to wash fruits and vegetables thoroughly before eating them. This helps remove dirt, chemicals, bacteria, and other contaminants from the skins and outer layers of fruits and vegetables.

One of the benefits to eating organic isn't a benefit to your body at all but a benefit to the planet. Organic farming puts important nutrients back into the soil, while conventional farming can add contaminating chemicals to the soil and water.

ACCORDING TO RECENT STUDIES, 78% OF FAMILIES IN THE UNITED STATES BUY SOME FOOD THAT IS LABELED "ORGANIC."

PREMIUM QUALITY
ORGANIC
CERTIFIED PRODUCT

Because organic livestock, such as cows, are fed mostly grass and alfalfa, they usually have higher levels of omega-3 fatty acids, which are linked to healthier hearts in people who regularly eat them.

Organic produce is food grown with a sustainable, environmentally friendly focus, without using synthetic fertilizers or most conventional pesticides. Organic animal products are those made from or by animals who are not given antibiotics or extra growth hormones.

The History of Exercise
Modern Times

Fit for a President

During the early part of the 20th century, President Theodore Roosevelt encouraged Americans to become more active. He loved to hike and horseback ride, and since he overcame childhood asthma with exercise, he felt strongly about the importance of physical activity.

Jumpin' Jack Flash

The jumping jack was developed in the 20th century by a military general named John J. Pershing. The story goes that Pershing, while a cadet at West Point Military Academy, developed the jumping jack as a way to punish a fellow student.

GET INTO FIGHTING SHAPE

Many American men were drafted to serve in World War I. However, one-third of the people drafted were found physically unfit for the military. The government later passed laws that improved school physical education programs.

Make a Run for It

While the first treadmill was developed and used in ancient Roman times, Dr. Robert Bruce from the University of Washington introduced the first modern medical treadmill in 1952. Dr. Bruce was a cardiologist who used the treadmill to diagnose heart diseases and conditions. He used his research to develop the Bruce Protocol, which is a test that evaluates heart function and is still used today.

Can't Keep Up

In the late 1940s and early 1950s, tests were done on American and European children to check their physical fitness. More than half of the American children tested failed the test, which included doing sit-ups and toe touches. Because of this, President Eisenhower formed the President's Council on Physical Fitness, later renamed the President's Council of Physical Fitness and Sports, which established the President's Physical Fitness Award.

P.E. = Positive Effects

In the 21st century, most states don't mandate a set amount of time spent in physical education (P.E.) classes. In 2003, only 28% of high school students took P.E. daily, down from 42% only 10 years earlier. However, the recommended guidelines state that elementary school students should have at least 150 minutes of P.E. each week. This number goes up to 225 minutes for middle schoolers. So get out there and move—it does your body good!

Brain Maze

Think It Through

The human brain looks like it has hills and valleys over its surface. See if you can navigate up, down, and around the uneven terrain of the brain to get from one side to the other!

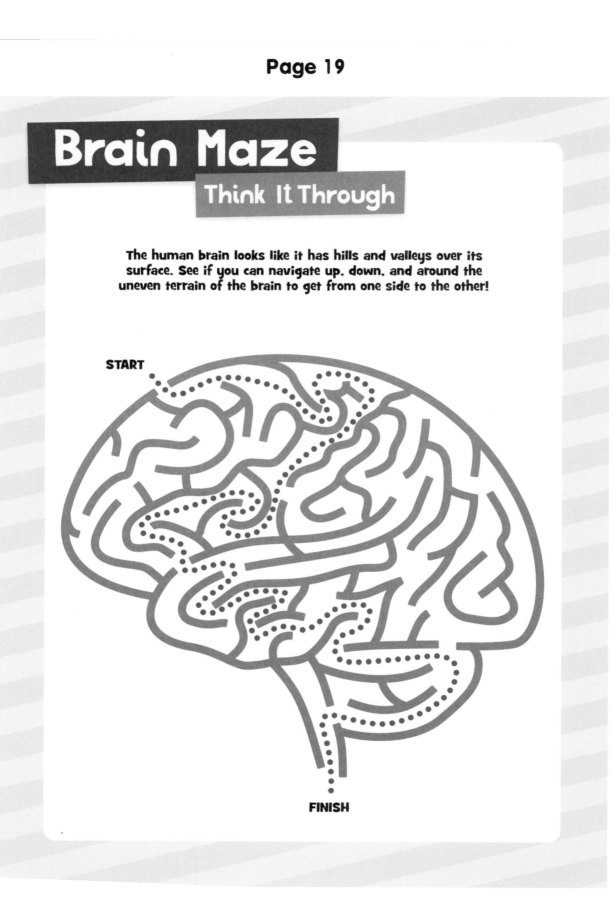

START

FINISH

Answers

Page 29

Spot the Difference
Dinnertime

Find and circle 10 differences between these two pictures of a family about to eat a big meal.

Spot the Difference

Twin-tastic

Find and circle 10 differences between these two pictures of sets of twins and their friends having fun in the park.

Intestine Maze

Digesting Food

The intestines are the organs in which the majority of digestion takes place. Help dinner move through the intestines to get from one end to the other.

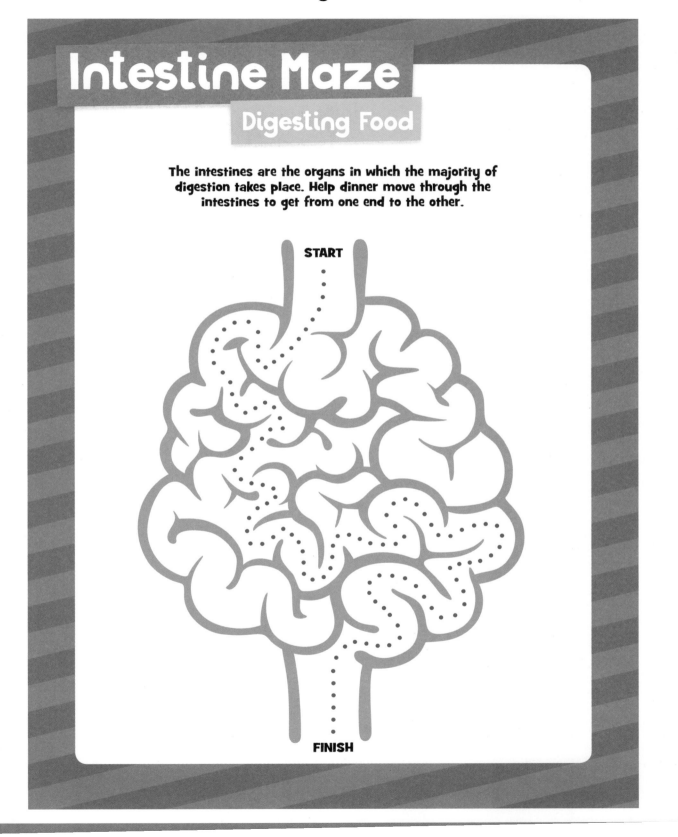

START

FINISH

Fill in the Blanks

Taste Test

**Fill in the missing letters to complete the facts below.
For help, look at the opposite page about taste.**

Taste buds are **S E N S O R Y** cells.

Taste buds are located on your tongue, as well as in your
T H R O A T and on the roof of your **M O U T H**.

You **L O S E** about half of your taste buds by age 60.

P A P I L L A E are the small
bumps on which your taste buds sit.

The five basic tastes are: **S W E E T**, **B I T T E R**,
S O U R, **S A L T Y**, and **S A V O R Y**.

Another word for "savory" is **U M A M I**.

A reduced sense of taste is called
H Y P O G E U S I A.

Someone with no sense of taste has **A G E U S I A**.

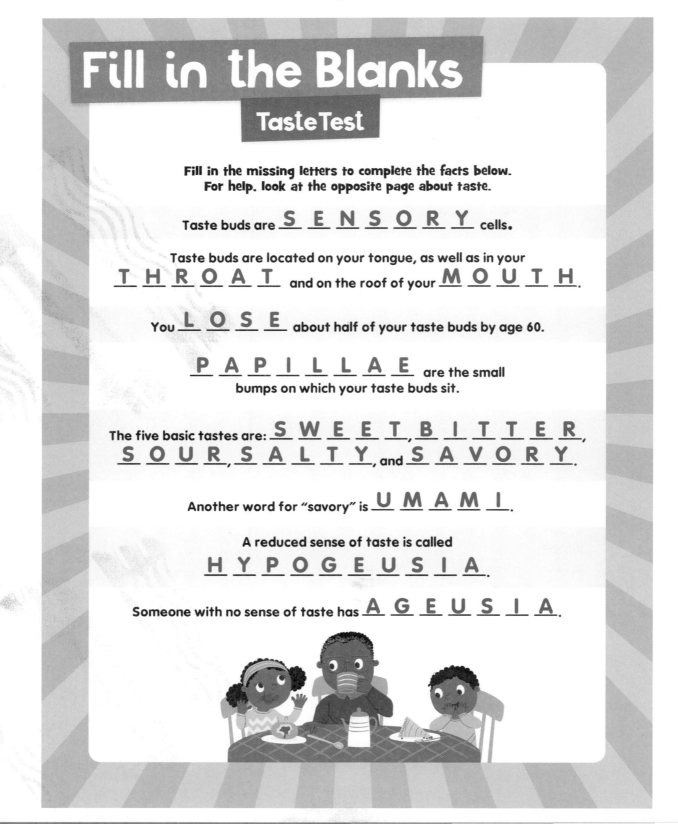

Crossword Puzzle
Exercise

Complete the crossword using the clues below.
For help, look at the pages about exercise.

ACROSS

2. Having fun, like at the playground

5. Chemicals released by the body during exercise

7. Moving faster than walking

9. Moving your body, usually for better health

11. Human tissue that works together to produce movement

12. Part of the body where sweat is made and released

DOWN

1. People who can touch their toes are said to have this

3. The ability to perform a movement, like exercise, for a long period of time

4. A form of exercise that uses different ways of breathing and movement, or poses

6. Having this allows you to lift heavy objects

8. To extend your arms and legs

10. Another name for perspiration

Word Scramble

Global Foods

Unscramble the letters to find words about healthy things for your body, healthy food from other places, and where to find them. For help, look at the opposite page.

MAVSTINI
V I T A M I N S

OUNCCOT
C O C O N U T

CTMUERRI
T U R M E R I C

OAKL
K O L A

MURICCNU
C U R C U M I N

DAYRTHE
H Y D R A T E

SALIMAYA
M A L A Y S I A

AULMCIC
C A L C I U M

ADITALHN
T H A I L A N D

CRAIFA
A F R I C A

ROLSTETLECEY
E L E C T R O L Y T E S

Word Search
Systems of the Body

Look at the puzzle below and see if you can find these words all about the digestive and lymphatic systems. Circle the words going across, up and down, and diagonally. Some words may be backwards!

ABSORB	GALLBLADDER	LYMPHATIC
BILE	ILEUM	NODES
CHYME	INTESTINE	SPLEEN
DIGEST	JEJUNUM	STOMACH
DUODENUM	LIVER	WASTE

```
S E D O N D N D Q K L C D O N
C K Z O B C U C A N I I K M D
I P P S E O N N O E V B W T W
F N R H D Z S T M L E X U A W
J E T E K B B Y K Y Y R J S M O
R M N E R O H V W M B T G H Y
T U U O S C Q U V P E I W H G
M D S N J T T B S H N L N X I
E B H A U E I H C A M O T S H
A D P I Y J N N G T M T N F H
C N S P L E E N E I L S P M J
L N V A V E X J T C V E C B L
K I F T T V U H G G O G L A E
F X S B G V P M H A G I K I D
G A L L B L A D D E R D S U B
```

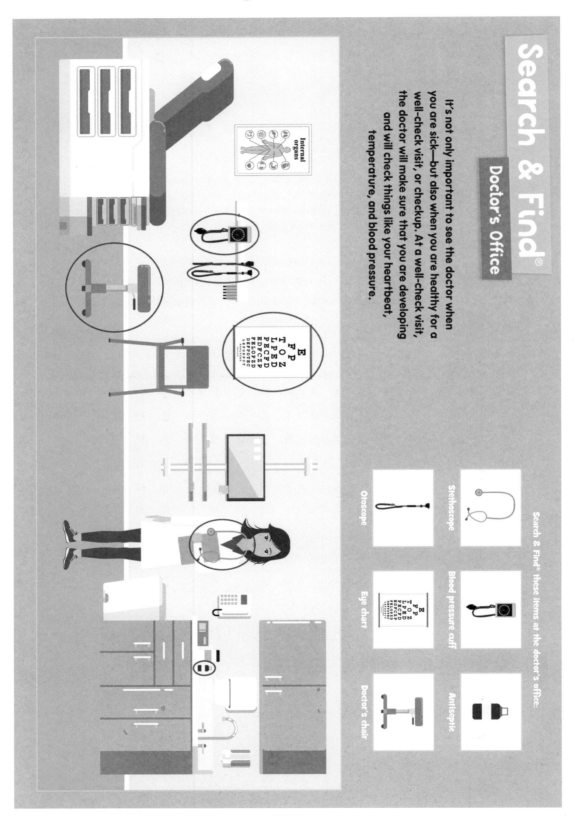

Search & Find®

Doctor's Office

It's not only important to see the doctor when you are sick—but also when you are healthy for a well-check visit, or checkup. At a well-check visit, the doctor will make sure that you are developing and will check things like your heartbeat, temperature, and blood pressure.

Internal organs

Search & Find® these items at the doctor's office:

Stethoscope

Blood pressure cuff

Antiseptic

Otoscope

Eye chart

Doctor's chair

Word Search
Nutrition

Look at the puzzle below and see if you can find these words all about nutrition. Circle the words going across, up and down, and diagonally. Some words may be backwards!

CALORIES	HYDRATE	SNACK
ENERGY	MEAL	STARCH
FAT	MINERAL	SUGAR
FOOD	PORTION	VITAMIN
FUEL	PROTEIN	WATER

```
L H E Q X O X H R C V F O O D
C B Y X A J G Y C I K D G G R
U G S D M M A A T R S E D N Z
Q K V R R D I A M D A N Z T N
J N P A L A M N F I C T S N O
E B R G Y I T X E C F H S R I
N H O U N W C E E R A U E L T
I V T S Y G R E N E A T E P R
S D E O B H W E S W A L L O
G C I S C I X N T W A Z K D P
L P N J S N A M J Z R K L F M
V A D B L C M V B E E Z E A H
N X E B K P S V X G S B Q T W
D B Y M V Q T A R E D Z T Z S
C A L O R I E S K Y T E M V M
```

Crossword Puzzle
Headaches

Complete the crossword using the clues below.
For help, look at the pages of headache facts!

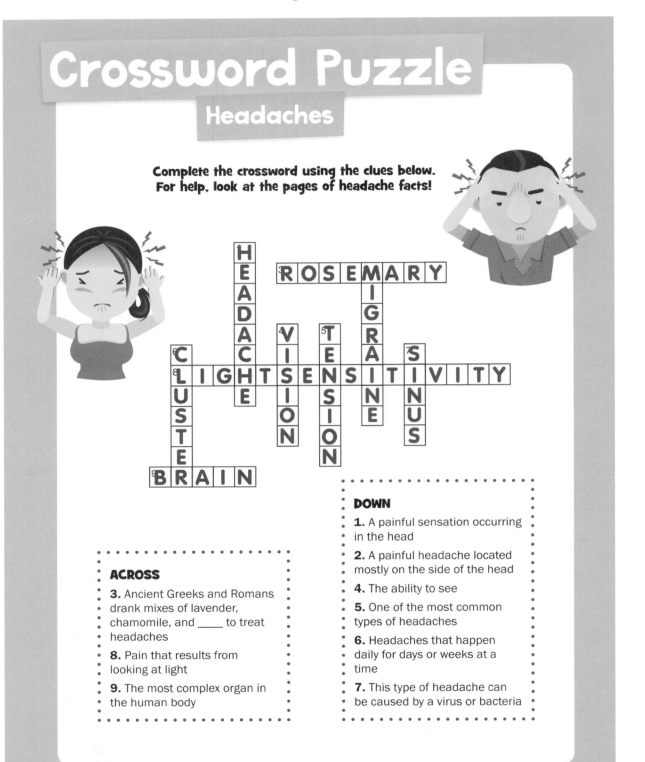

ACROSS

3. Ancient Greeks and Romans drank mixes of lavender, chamomile, and _____ to treat headaches

8. Pain that results from looking at light

9. The most complex organ in the human body

DOWN

1. A painful sensation occurring in the head

2. A painful headache located mostly on the side of the head

4. The ability to see

5. One of the most common types of headaches

6. Headaches that happen daily for days or weeks at a time

7. This type of headache can be caused by a virus or bacteria

Crossword Puzzle
Twins

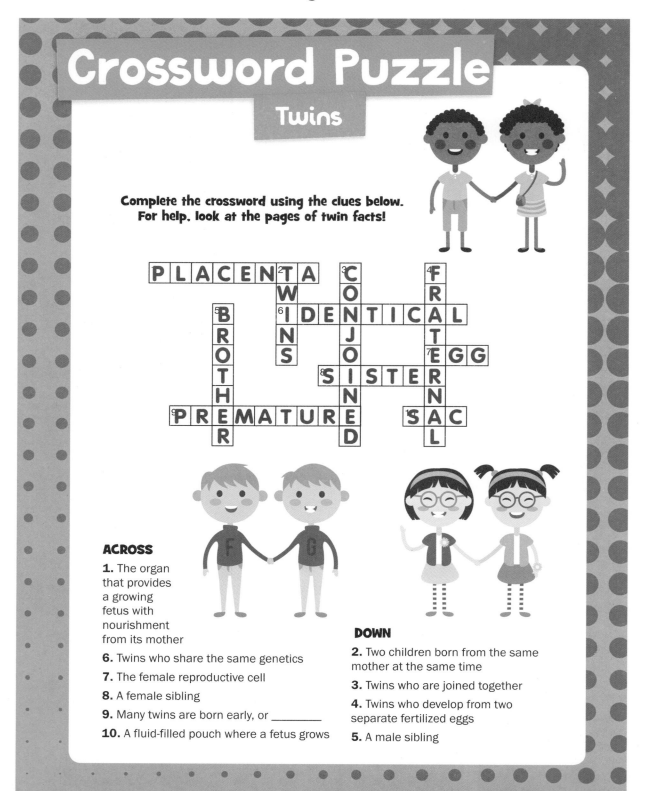

Complete the crossword using the clues below.
For help, look at the pages of twin facts!

```
P L A C E N T A      C          F
        W            O          R
    B   I D E N T I C A L       A
    R   N            J          T
    O   S        S I S T E R     E G G
    T          8  N              R
    H   P R E M A T U R E D      S A C
    E              E   D          A
    R                             L
```

ACROSS

1. The organ that provides a growing fetus with nourishment from its mother

6. Twins who share the same genetics

7. The female reproductive cell

8. A female sibling

9. Many twins are born early, or _____

10. A fluid-filled pouch where a fetus grows

DOWN

2. Two children born from the same mother at the same time

3. Twins who are joined together

4. Twins who develop from two separate fertilized eggs

5. A male sibling

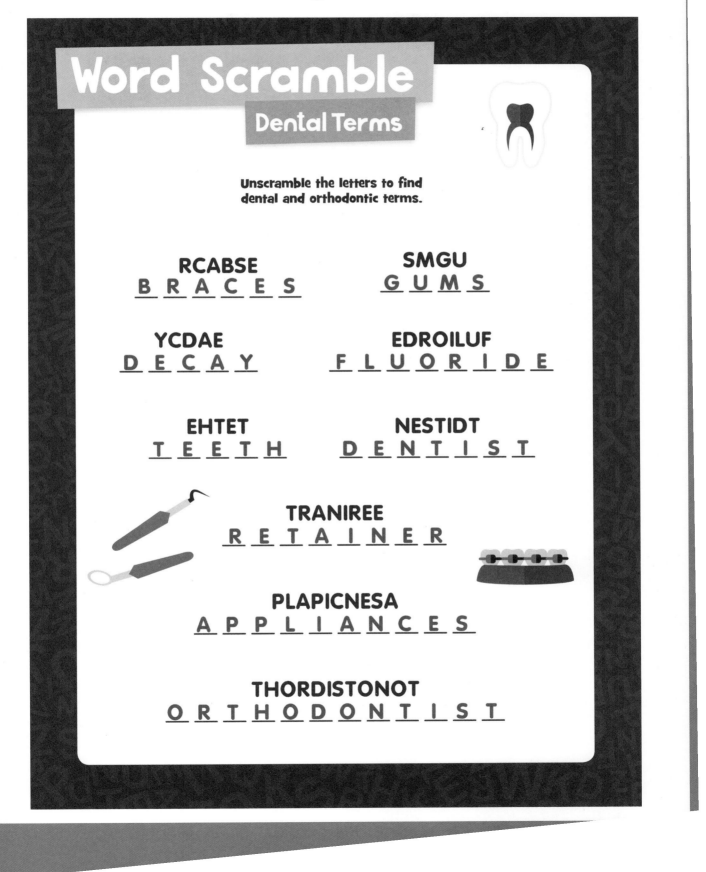

Word Scramble
Dental Terms

Unscramble the letters to find
dental and orthodontic terms.

RCABSE
B R A C E S

SMGU
G U M S

YCDAE
D E C A Y

EDROILUF
F L U O R I D E

EHTET
T E E T H

NESTIDT
D E N T I S T

TRANIREE
R E T A I N E R

PLAPICNESA
A P P L I A N C E S

THORDISTONOT
O R T H O D O N T I S T

Fill in the Blanks

Exercise in Ancient Times

**Fill in the missing letters to complete the facts below.
For help, look at the previous pages about the history of exercise.**

Prehistoric people found their food by **H U N T I N G**
and **G A T H E R I N G**.

This Chinese philosopher, **C O N F U C I U S**,
encouraged physical fitness to increase health.

This was the ancient Greek version of a physical trainer:
P A I D O T R I B E.

The ancient Greek civilization of **S P A R T A**
highly valued physical fitness in both men and women.

Yoga literally translates to this word: **U N I O N**.

Multiple ancient civilizations enjoyed practicing and
playing the same sports, like: **W R E S T L I N G**
and **G Y M N A S T I C S**.

The goal of yoga is to achieve **B A L A N C E** with nature.

Crossword Puzzle
Kidney Stones

Complete the crossword using the clues below.
For help, look at the opposite page.

ACROSS

2. To help prevent kidney stones, avoid eating too much food with sugar or ____

5. This is one risk factor for kidney stones

8. You need to drink enough of this to help avoid kidney stones

9. Large kidney stones can cause a person to feel this

DOWN

1. If a ____ member has kidney stones, you may be more likely to get them

3. Small kidney stones leave the body in this

4. Tiny crystals that are made of more waste than liquid

6. What kidney stones will do if they aren't removed from the body

7. Stones cause backups in this system of the body

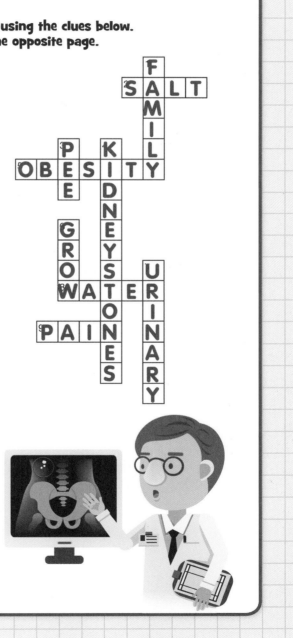

Fill in the Blanks

Ligaments

Fill in the missing letters to complete the facts below.
For help, look at the previous pages about ligaments.

Ligaments provide stability for J O I N T S.

A sprained A N K L E is actually a torn ligament,

and it commonly occurs in sports that include jumping.

Elbow ligaments can be damaged by repeated motions in this sport:
B A S E B A L L.

There are two kinds of ligaments in the elbow: the U L N A R
and L A T E R A L collateral ligaments.

Ligaments in this part of the body connect to the arm and
to the collarbone: S H O U L D E R.

If you sprain a ligament, you should avoid putting
W E I G H T on that area.

Ligaments connect B O N E S in your body.

Page 259

Word Search
Physical Activity

Look at the puzzle below and see if you can find these words all about physical activity. Circle the words going across, up and down, and diagonally. Some words may be backwards!

EXERTION   PEDOMETER   STRENGTH
METABOLISM   PILATES   TRAINING
MUSCLES   RECOVERY   ULTRAMARATHON
OLYMPICS   RESISTANCE   WALKING
OXYGEN   RUNNING   WEIGHTS

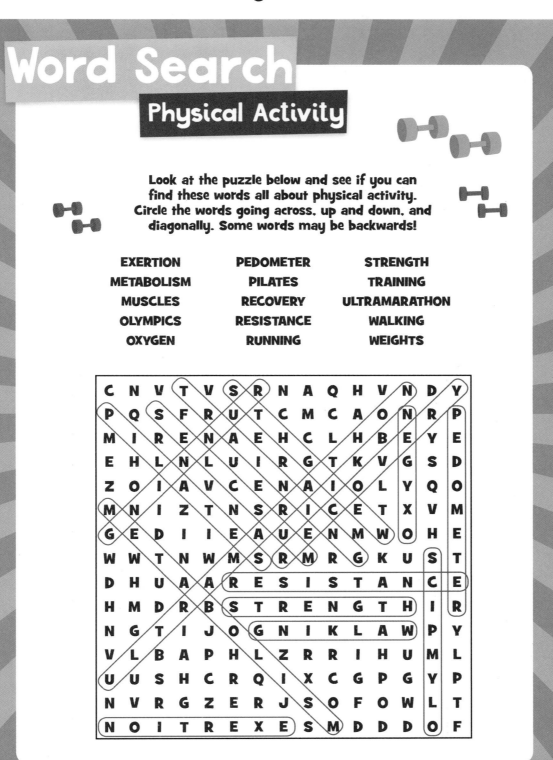

```
C N V T V S R N A Q H V N D Y
P Q S F R U T C M C A O N R P
M I R E N A E H C L H B E Y E
E H L N L U I R G T K V G S D
Z O I A V C E N A I O L Y Q O
M N I Z T N S R I C E T X V M
G E D I I E A U E N M W O H E
W W T N W M S R M R G K U S T
D H U A A R E S I S T A N C E
H M D R B S T R E N G T H I R
N G T I J O G N I K L A W P Y
V L B A P H L Z R R I H U M L
U U S H C R Q I X C G P G Y P
N V R G Z E R J S O F O W L T
N O I T R E X E S M D D D O F
```

Word Search
Dental Hygiene

Look at the puzzle below and see if you can find these words all about dental hygiene. Circle the words going across, up and down, and diagonally. Some words may be backwards!

BACTERIA   DENTURES   MOUTHWASH
BRISTLES   FILLING   PLAQUE
CAVITY   FLOSS   TEETH
DECAY   FLUORIDE   TOOTHBRUSH
DENTIST   HYGIENIST   TOOTHPASTE

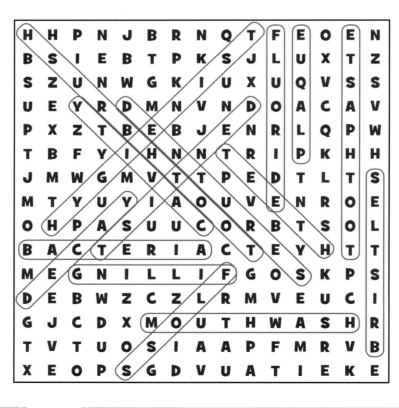

H H P N J B R N Q T F E O E N
B S I E B T P K S J L U X T Z
S Z U N W G K I U X U Q V S S
U E Y R D M N V N D O A C A V
P X Z T B E B J E N R L Q P W
T B F Y I H N N T R I P K H H
J M W G M V T T P E D T L T S
M T Y U Y I A O U V E N R O E
O H P A S U U C O R B T S O L
B A C T E R I A C T E Y H T T
M E G N I L L I F G O S K P S
D E B W Z C Z L R M V E U C I
G J C D X M O U T H W A S H R
T V T U O S I A A P F M R V B
X E O P S G D V U A T I E K E

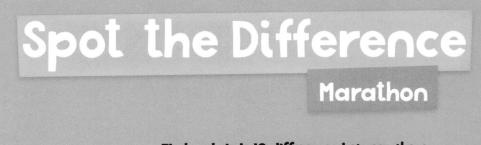

Spot the Difference

Marathon

Find and circle 10 differences between these two pictures of people running a marathon.

Page 287

Fill in the Blanks
Hormones

Fill in the missing letters to complete the facts below. For help, look at the pages about hormones and puberty.

HORMONES are different in men and women and affect everything from how much hair they have on their bodies to how their bones are shaped.

ANDROGENS are the type of hormone responsible for hair growth.

High levels of **ESTROGEN** cause a woman's bones to harden before a man's bones harden.

A woman's bones are set by the time she is **18** years old, but a man's bones aren't set until he is **21** years old.

The shorter your right pointer finger is relative to your right ring finger, the more **TESTOSTERONE** you were exposed to before birth.

In both boys and girls, the **PITUITARY** gland produces hormones when puberty begins.

The hormones that cause puberty also cause **ACNE**, or pimples, to appear because of increased oil production during puberty.

Answers

Pair Matching

Skeletons

There are 3 sets of skeletons below. Draw a line to connect the skeleton on the left with its identical twin on the right.

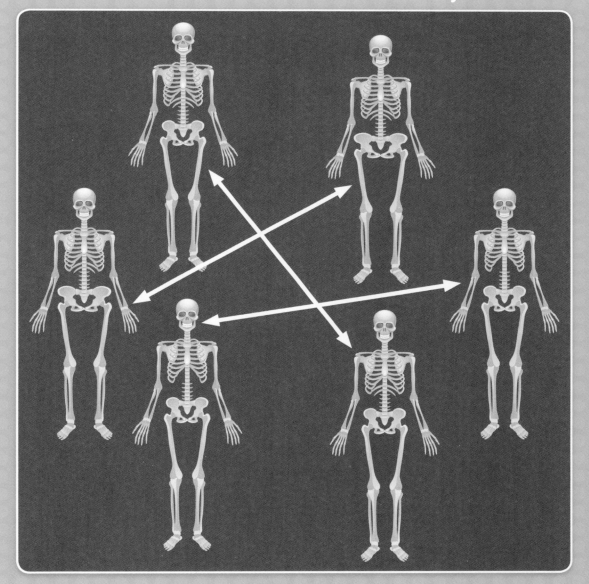